The River Boyne we then did wade,
   having possest the other Shore:
The Rebells then we sprawling laid,
   they never found the like before:
Horse and Foot did boldly venture,
   being strangers unto fear:
Still as we fir'd, they retir'd,
   thus our Foes we soon did clear.

Queen.

My Royal Lord, reply'd the Queen,
   thou was't expos'd to Dangers great,
Where nought but Fire and Smoak was seen
   yet Providence on thee did wait:
And preserv'd thy life in Battel,
   where great numbers did lye slain:
This is my blessing, I'm possessing
   of my dearest Lord again.

King.

Although my Army won the Day,
   and foes on us their backs they turn'd;
Yet warlike Schomberg in the Fray
   was kill'd, for whom I'm much concern'd:

O that brave Couragious Heroe
   likewise Valiant VValker too:
Though they expir'd, when they fir'd,
   France shall one Day for it rue.

Queen.

Alas! that sad surprizing News
   did grieve each loyal Subject here:
And did their senses so amuse,
   none could forbear to shed a tear:
Many brave couragious Souldiers
   near the River Boyne was slain:
Yet this great blessing, I'm possessing,
   to enjoy my Lord again.

Cast by thy weary Armour bright,
   receive thy Scepter, Crown and Ball:
With Lords and Nobles take delight,
   thou being King and Lord of all:
Thou on Englands throne art seated,
   Subjects with a happy Reign,
This is a blessing, I'm possessing,
   to embrace my Lord again.

printed by and for J. Millet, at the Angel in Little-Brittain : Where Countrey Chapmen may be furnish'd with all sorts of New and Old small Books and Ballads at reasonable rates.

The Life and Times of
WILLIAM AND MARY

OVERLEAF LEFT Sir John Thornhill's ceiling
in the Painted Hall at Greenwich: the
centre panel showing William and Mary,
and their plan for the Chapel.
OVERLEAF RIGHT A canvas bag
embroidered with beads by Queen Mary
for her husband.

The Life and Times of
WILLIAM AND MARY

John Miller

Introduction by Antonia Fraser

Book Club Associates, London

Series design by Paul Watkins
Layout by Margaret Fraser and Juanita Grout

Filmset by Keyspools Limited, Golborne, Lancashire
Printed and bound in Great Britain by
Morrison & Gibb Ltd, London & Edinburgh

Contents

Introduction

WHEN MARY STUART, niece of Charles II, was first told she was to marry her first cousin William of Orange, she 'wept for a day and a half'. Yet not only was the union to prove a happy one domestically, but it was also fateful in dynastic terms: for it brought together the head of the Dutch quasi-royal House with a potential claimant to the English throne. It thus gave a focus for those who were becoming disenchanted with the Stuart regime and who were looking for alternatives. Before long, Mary would be called upon to stand by her husband against her own father.

The year 1688 was a critical one in British history. Mary's father, James II, had forfeited virtually all support by his arbitrary, above all his Catholic, policies. Protestants feared James at home; abroad they feared the power of the strongest Catholic ruler, Louis XIV. It was to William – now through marriage at least arguably a successor to the throne, and, as leader of the Dutch Republic, France's most implacable enemy – that they looked. William's own motives were clear enough: quite apart from his own ambitions a successful *coup* would bring England into line against France. And so in November, he landed at Torbay proclaiming his intention to summon a free Parliament and restore the nation's lost liberties.

Thus began a new era. In the year that followed, a new constitution took shape through a series of acts which limited the monarchy and, as John Miller emphasises, through Parliament's determination to keep control of the purse strings. It was not a status that appealed to William. He had wanted to rule by himself, and joint rule, with Mary, was forced on him by Parliament. Many Englishmen had indeed wanted Mary to reign alone, though here they met a blank refusal. How could a husband obey his wife when the natural order demanded the opposite? Mary declared that 'she did not know that the laws of England were so contrary to the laws of God'. So joint rule it was: and as for the other limitations William accepted them only with the greatest reluctance, complaining that 'the Commons used him like a dog'. It must have been a rude shock to discover that, far from escaping from the kind of restrictions he had encountered in the Dutch Republic, he was now compelled to pioneer the first effectively limited monarchy in his new homeland.

Mary died in 1694. Her totally blameless life and selfless devotion to her duties won her the affection of her people. Evelyn wrote, 'In sum she was an admirable woman' fit for comparison with 'the renowned Queen Elizabeth'. William was less widely mourned when he died eight years later. 'No king can have been less lamented than this has been,' wrote one contemporary. Yet William too was selfless, and his achievements were remarkable. Abroad he guided British policy in the direction which would lead, in the next reign, to the glorious victories of Marlborough; in Ireland, he intervened decisively with his victory of the battle of the Boyne in 1690, completing a process of conquest begun as long ago as the age of Elizabeth; at home he adjusted – admittedly not enthusiastically – to an entirely new concept of kingship as his country groped uneasily towards the compromises of constitutional monarchy. Mary's contribution may have been merely reflected in the success of her husband: her comfort, love and moral support helped him to use his talents to the full. But it was together, as John Miller delineates in a study remarkable for its able exposition of both politics and personalities, that they made the 'Glorious Revolution' work.

Antonia Fraser

Acknowledgments

Photographs and illustrations were supplied or are reproduced by kind permission of the following.

The pictures on pages 47, 148–9, *163*, 172, are reproduced by gracious permission of H.M. the Queen; on page 75 by kind permission of the Duke of Buccleuch and Queensberry; on page 83 by kind permission of the Earl of Jersey. The Governor and Company of the Bank of England: 186/1, 186/2, 187; British Museum: 98–9, 118, 152, 208; Department of the Environment, Crown Copyright: *2*, 154, 154–5, 155, 170–1, *174*, *174–5*, *175*, 215; Frans Halsmuseum, Haarlem: *50*; Haags Gemeentemuseum, The Hague: 38–9; London Museum: *3*; Mansell Collection: 18, 64, 101, 106, 138–9, 146, 196–7; Mary Evans Picture Library: 75, 176, 177; Mauritshuis, The Hague: *14*, *81*; National Maritime Museum: *62–3*; National Portrait Gallery: 41, 64, 69, 71, 82, 88, 127, 159, *162*, 182, 183, 207/2, 212; Public Record Office: 91; Radio Times Hulton Picture Library: 16–17, 26, 30–1, 44–5, 58, 66–7, 74, 78, 79, 86, 87, 88–9, 89, 98–9, 104–5, 112, 124–5, 136–7,142–3, 145, 152–3, 156–7, 160, 167, 169, 191, 192, 204, 205, 209, 210, 213; Rijksmuseum, Amsterdam: 10–11, 13, 21, 24–5, 33, 34–5, 42, *50–1*, 58–9, 59, 60–1, *84*, 94–5, 116–17, 179, 180; Stichting Johan Maurits van Nassau, The Hague: *15*; Victoria and Albert Museum: 29, 48, 54, 60, *93/1*, *93/2*, *96/1*, *96/2*, 109, 110, 111, 121, 122, 132, 132–3, 133, 151, 164/1, 164/2, 165, 166, 193, 199, 200, 201, 207/1, 216.

Acknowledgments are also due to the photographers Sally Chappell and A.C. Cooper Ltd.

Numbers in italics indicate colour illustrations.

Picture research by Pat Hodgson.

Maps drawn by Design Practitioners Ltd.

A NOTE ON DATES

In the seventeenth century most of Europe had adopted the more accurate Gregorian calendar, while England retained the old Julian calendar. As a result there was a discrepancy between English and foreign dating of ten days (eleven after 1700). For the sake of simplicity I have used the English style of dating at all times, but with the year starting on 1 January rather than 25 March.   J.M.

1 The Orange

Inheritance 1650-72

IN OCTOBER 1650 William II, Prince of Orange, stayed at his hunting-lodge at Dieren, near Arnhem. Despite the cold, wet weather he hunted daily, but on the 17th he retired early, complaining that he felt ill. Next day he had a fever and his doctors soon diagnosed smallpox. On the 27th he died. For some time no one dared to tell his wife Mary, the daughter of Charles I of England. She was already well over eight months pregnant and it was feared that the shock might cause her to miscarry. As it was, the last days of her pregnancy were hardly easy. She had to receive formal condolences from the States General, the States of Holland and the city of Amsterdam. She was harassed by her mother-in-law, Amalia von Solms, whose secretary Huygens tried to make her write in person to inform the rulers of Europe of her husband's death. Her confinement took place in a room hung with black; all the women were in mourning and she had to endure Amalia's unwelcome company for hour after hour. At 2.30 p.m. on 4 November (her nineteenth birthday) she fell into labour; six hours later a son was born. Mary wanted to call him Charles, after her father and brother, but Amalia insisted that he should have the good Orange name of William Henry; after a long struggle, Amalia got her way.

As head of the illustrious House of Orange, William's inheritance was a great yet peculiar one. The princes of Orange traditionally held the greatest offices in the Dutch republic. This small but remarkable state had won its independence from Spain, then the greatest power in Europe, after a struggle lasting eighty years and had developed into the leading maritime and trading nation. The republic was a federation of seven of the seventeen provinces of the Low Countries which had come under Habsburg rule; the other ten remained in Spanish hands. Each province retained its own laws and customs, had its own representative assembly or states and sent a delegation to the States General of the United Provinces. The provinces were not equally powerful. The province of Holland, which contained the great towns of Amsterdam, Rotterdam and Leyden, was far richer than any of the others and contributed fifty-eight per cent of the common budget. Holland's delegation to the States General was often able to carry its wishes against those of the six other provinces. This was possible because the constitutions of both the States General and the provincial states required

12

decisions to be unanimous, at least on major issues. As a result, Holland could, in practice, exercise a veto in the States General and a single great town (usually Amsterdam) could do the same in the States of Holland. Each province had a permanent official called a pensionary to resolve disputes and prevent deadlocks. The pensionary of Holland also had considerable influence in the States General.

The wealth of the republic, and especially of Holland, came from trade, and power lay mainly with the towns. These were ruled by oligarchies of 'regents', who served for life and filled vacancies by co-option. There was clearly a danger that such bodies might become closed and corrupt. This happened later, but was less common in the seventeenth century when many town councils were prepared to open their ranks to men of talent and public spirit and showed themselves very sensitive to

R. de Hooghe's engraving of the birth of William III, an event that was marred by tragedy and discord within the Orange family, but enthusiastically celebrated by the people of Holland.

13

ABOVE Gerrit Honthorst's painting of the
stadholder Prince Frederick Henry and his wife
Amalia von Solms, the grandparents of William III.
Friction between the dominating Amalia and
her hostile daughter-in-law Mary Stuart caused
much unhappiness in the Orange family.

RIGHT William II, who died shortly before his son's
birth: a portrait by Gerrit Honthorst. William had
given active support to the Stuart cause, in the
person of Charles I, and had been much liked by
his brother-in-law Charles II.

The Hague in the seventeenth century: this engraving is taken from a view painted by Clement de Jonghe in 1621, which shows the Mauritshuis.

public opinion: the republic had the highest level of literacy and the freest Press in Europe, and the regents, unlike most aristocracies, lived in close proximity to the ordinary citizens. In practice, therefore, the regents showed a large measure of both talent and responsibility. This was just as well, for there was always a danger that the republic's cumbersome constitutional machinery might seize up altogether. As it was, the system could not really provide the quick and decisive action which was necessary in wartime. For this, the republic had traditionally looked to the princes of Orange.

The princes of Orange were by far the richest citizens of the republic. They had great estates throughout the Netherlands

and in Germany. They were sovereign princes in their own right, deriving their title from the tiny principality of Orange, on the Rhône near Avignon. Their outlook was therefore more international than that of most Dutchmen. Their Court, where French was usually spoken, was modest by the standards of most European rulers but seemed alien and extravagant to the frugal Dutch. Besides being rich, they were also very talented: William the Silent, Maurice of Nassau, Frederick Henry and William III were all great military and political leaders. Without them the republic could not have won and maintained its independence. Their wealth and talent gave them a natural claim to leadership but they held their great offices as servants of

17

Leven en Daden der vijf Princen van Orangie.

WILLEM DE I PRINS VAN ORANIE.

MAVRITZ PRINS VAN ORANIE.

WILLEM DE III CONINCK VAN GROOT BRITTANIEN VRANCKRYCK EN YRLANT & PRINS VAN ORANIEN

FREDERIK HENRIK PRINS VAN ORANIE.

WILLEM DE II PRINS VAN ORANIE.

the republic. First they were stadholders, or lieutenants, of the various provinces, although no prince of Orange ever held all seven stadholderates. The official powers of the office were limited, concerned mostly with law and order. However the office conferred considerable authority which could be used informally to influence the states of weaker provinces like Gelderland; such influence reinforced that stemming from the family's great wealth and prestige. Secondly, the princes were appointed to the offices of captain general and admiral general and so commanded the army and navy of the United Provinces. Besides all this the House of Orange enjoyed vast popular support – far more than the regents ever did – and could usually count on the backing, in the pulpit and elsewhere, of the clergy of the Dutch Reformed Church.

The princes of Orange thus exercised quasi-royal power but without the title of king. William III's experience of the office of stadholder was reflected both in his belief that high office carried an obligation of service and in his concern with the reality of power rather than its outward forms: power was to be used for a constructive purpose, it was not an end in itself. The offices of stadholder and captain general were not hereditary but had always been granted to the head of the House of Orange. During the seventeenth century, however (which was, after all, the heyday of monarchy), some regents began to fear that the princes of Orange planned to set themselves up as kings. When William III's grandfather, Frederick Henry, married his son to Mary Stuart in 1641 he laid great stress on her royal birth and clearly hoped that her father would help him to establish an Orange monarchy. As it was, the Stuart connection proved a liability, and relations between the House of Orange and the regents of Holland reached a new low in 1650, when William II attempted a military *coup* against Amsterdam.

The offices of stadholder and captain general lapsed with William II's death. Most Dutchmen expected his young son to succeed to them in due course, but many regents now felt that the two offices, the civil and the military, conferred too much power and should not both be granted to one man. Undoubtedly a measure of oligarchic self-interest and perverse localism underlay this belief, but there was also a measure of patriotism and republican idealism. The respect for provincial

OPPOSITE 'The illustrious House of Orange': this contemporary engraving shows its members, from William the Silent to William III.

and municipal rights lay at the root of the liberty and tolerance
of Dutch society and it was reasonable to fear that these would
suffer if a centralised monarchy were established. The States
party, as the opponents of the House of Orange were called, also
feared that William might try to use the power of his Stuart
relations to strengthen his position in the republic, as his father
and grandfather had hoped to do. Thus men like Pensionary
Johan de Witt, the leading figure in the States of Holland, saw
themselves as defending Dutch liberty and institutions against
foreign interference and the alien aspirations of the House of
Orange. It was therefore by no means certain that William
would inherit the offices of his ancestors. The struggle of
William and his supporters, who controlled several of the
smaller provinces, to secure his elevation to these offices was a
central feature of Dutch politics in the dozen or so years before
1672. This struggle had a formative influence on William's
character and political outlook and illustrated clearly both his
ruthlessness and his practicality.

William's childhood was characterised by both personal unhappiness and expectations of future greatness. An example of
this was his christening in January 1651, at the Great Church at
The Hague. His mother refused to come after her row with
Amalia about his name, and the church was still hung with
black in mourning for his father. But the crowd was so great
that the choir, disconcerted, sang out of tune and the noise
forced the preacher to abandon his sermon. To the annoyance
of the regents, the christening robe was trimmed with royal
ermine. The feud between Mary and Amalia continued but
once they had resolved their quarrel over his guardianship it
had little direct effect on William. He spent more time with his
mother than was usual in royal families, which gave him a certain emotional stability even if it did him little good politically.
Mary was always a Stuart first and foremost. She thought her
main duty was to help restore her brother Charles to the
English throne; then, and only then, he could use his power to
have William raised to his rightful dignities. She lent, or rather
gave, her impoverished brother money which her son could ill
afford and paid little attention to Dutch affairs, which at least
meant that she did William's interests little positive harm.
Furiously proud of her royal birth, she made no secret of her

The Netherlands

in the second half of
the seventeenth century

The United Provinces
independent of the Empire since 1648

Spanish Netherlands

Acquired by France from
Spanish Netherlands 1659-79

The Empire

NORTH SEA

GRONINGEN

Groningen
Leeuwarden
FRIESLAND
DRENTHE

Texel

HOLLAND
Hoorn
Alkmaar
Haarlem
ZUIDER ZEE
Kampen
OVERYSSEL
Amsterdam
Zutphen
Leyden
UTRECHT
GELDERLAND
Scheveningen
Ryswick   Utrecht
Dieren
The Hague   Delft
Arnhem
Briel   Rotterdam   *R. Waal*
Nymegen
Dordrecht
ZEELAND   Grave
CLEVES
Middelburg   Breda
SPANISH
Walcheren   THE GENERALITY   GELDER-
Flushing   LAND

MUNSTER

Ostend
Nieuwport   Antwerp
Dunkirk   Bruges   Ghent   BRABANT
Calais   Dixmude   Mechlin   JULICH   Cologne
FLANDERS   Ypres   Oudenarde   Louvain   Maastricht
St Omer   Courtrai   Brussels   Landen   Aix-la-Chapelle
Lille   Tournai   Enghien   BISHOPRIC OF LIÉGE
Bouvines   Steenkerk
ARTOIS   Condé   Mons   Seneffe   Liége   Limburg
Arras   Valenciennes   Namur   Spa   LIMBURG   Nassau
Cambrai   HAINAUT   Charlerol
R. Scheldt   *R. Rhine*
R. Sambre
R. Somme   *R. Moselle*

LUXEMBOURG

Amiens
PICARDY
LORRAINE
Sedan   Luxembourg
Soissons   Reims
FRANCE
R. Seine   *R. Meuse*   Verdun
Paris   CHAMPAGNE   Metz

loathing for the bourgeois Dutch and their republic: 'The greatest punishment of this world is to live all my life here', she wrote. The Dutch found her aloof and arrogant. She did, however, give William a mother's love, a commodity in short supply among princes, and an education that was intended to fit him for his future tasks as Prince of Orange.

From his earliest years, William's high status was clearly indicated. At two and a half he was given his own Court; at four he began to make public appearances and by the time he was nine he sometimes appeared alone. He was wildly popular and was cheered wherever he went. His formal education began a little later than his training as a public figure. When William was six Pastor Trigland began to instruct him in the Reformed faith and so laid the basis of William's deep and committed Calvinism. Not until he was nine did he start to study other subjects. His tutor Zuylestein, a bastard son of Frederick Henry, was rather lazy and not very cultivated, but he and his colleagues gave William an education that was designed to teach him to be a godly ruler. There was a firm foundation of religion. William was to read the Bible regularly, to go to church twice on Sundays and to answer questions afterwards in front of the servants. Next came languages: he had learned English from his mother and also spoke French, the language of the Court, Dutch, German, Latin and Spanish. His spelling and grammar were poor, but he got by. Thirdly, he was coached in public behaviour. He learned to overcome his natural shyness, to be polite and affable and to hide his real feelings. As Huygens said, 'He who is master of himself will be master of others.' All his life William rarely lost his temper in public, although he sometimes kicked his servants in private. He was also given a firm grounding in military theory and, above all, he was filled with a sense of the greatness and glory of the House of Orange. In short, his was an essentially practical training for one destined by his birth to be a soldier, diplomat and politician. Little time was spent on literature or the arts, although William did develop a lively interest in painting and architecture.

Like many of his family, William was not a healthy child. He was small, thin and pale with a slightly hunched back. He suffered all his life from asthma and a hacking cough. His diet was carefully regulated and he was not at first allowed to take much exercise; he ate and drank in moderation and went early to bed, habits which he kept up for most of his life and which were unusual in an age when most kings and nobles ate and drank enormously. His tutors also instilled in him a distrust of doctors which, considering the barbaric remedies they prescribed, can have done his health no harm. (Louis XIV's sufferings at the hands of his doctors were so harrowing and dramatic that the 'Sun King' liked to have an account of them read to him.) Like most of his class, William developed a passion for hunting: it gave him fresh air, which relieved his asthma, and rare moments of privacy, especially valuable for one brought up from infancy as a public figure. In general, however, his education encouraged him to put duty before pleasure and gave him a strong feeling of his family's rank and glory and of the rights and obligations that these entailed. His outward coldness and taciturnity and his firm self-control were reinforced by the harsh political experiences of his teens. As Burnet later wrote, 'He had observed the errors of too much talking more than those of too cold a silence.' By the age of nineteen he was precociously mature and self-possessed, as the French diplomat Pomponne later recalled:

> He was naturally intelligent and his judgment seemed as great as his intelligence. He knew how to hide his feelings – dissimulation seemed to come naturally to him. His morals were extremely regular. His manner was virtuous, calm and polite. He had an application and a capacity for business remarkable in one so young. He knew where his interests lay and how to manage them skilfully.

In 1660 the course of William's life changed abruptly. In May his uncle Charles was restored to the English throne. William met Charles and his brothers, the Dukes of York and Gloucester, at Delft and drove with them to The Hague, amid a din of bells and cannon. That evening a great dinner was held at the Mauritshuis, which the hungry Cavaliers doubtless enjoyed to the full. Cannon were fired after every toast and it was later calculated that the festivities and gifts to the new King and his family had cost over two million guilders. Later that year Mary pawned her jewels and went to enjoy the celebrations in England. While there she died of smallpox, depriving William of the only parent he had ever known. His mother's death and

The extravagant banquet given for Charles II (third from right) by the Dutch Government at the Mauritshuis in The Hague.

Charles's restoration changed his position. Thrown back on his own resources, he became even more composed and self-sufficient. His uncle's restoration made William a more considerable figure in the republic – in 1660 the States of Holland called him 'a worthy pawn and an instrument of great hope to the state'. But it also made his position more delicate. England was the republic's greatest commercial rival, and the regents also feared that William, like his father, might use English support in an effort to set himself up as a king. Charles was indeed anxious to support the pressure in the republic for

Louis XIV: his frequently expressed opinion was that he 'acknowledged no sovereignty of Orange to belong to the Prince . . . that it was his incontestably'.
The portrait is by Jean de la Haye.

26

William's elevation to the stadholderate, but for his own ends. If the pressure succeeded, Charles assumed that William would do as he told him; if it failed, England might still be able to exploit the divisions within the republic between the States party and the Orangists.

As William grew older, the pressure for his elevation increased. During the Anglo–Dutch war of 1665–7, William was declared a 'child of state' and the States of Holland took over responsibility for his education. This was a concession to the Orangists: the States could no longer treat William as a 'private person' and ignore all his claims to office. It was a heavy personal blow to William, however. His old tutors were dismissed; William was so upset at losing Zuylestein that he went in tears to beg the French ambassador to press for his reinstatement. But it was no use and William soon recovered his composure, bitterly criticising Amalia's mismanagement of his estates. De Witt himself now acted as William's tutor and saw him regularly. While gaining further experience of hiding his feelings, William may also have absorbed some of de Witt's learning and patriotism.

After the war, William took further steps towards gaining the titles which he had been brought up to regard as his by right. In 1668 he was declared First Noble of Zeeland and on his eighteenth birthday he took over the administration of his estates. Meanwhile, the foreign situation became increasingly menacing. In 1667 Louis XIV had attacked the Spanish Netherlands. His motives were twofold. In the short term he aimed to extend France's frontiers, to make them easier to defend. He was always surprisingly fearful of the dangers of invasion from both north and east. Ideally he would have liked to push the French frontiers back to the Rhine and the Meuse; at the least he wanted to rationalise his frontier with the Spanish Netherlands. At present this frontier was jagged, with French and Spanish fortified towns jumbled higgledy-piggledy. Louis and his strategic adviser, the great engineer Vauban, believed that only a linear frontier was really defensible. In the long term he hoped to seize some or all of the Spanish empire. The sickly King Carlos II had no children, and Louis's wife was one of the strongest claimants to the throne. While he waited for Carlos to die, Louis took advantage of the complex and varied laws of inheritance of the provinces of the Spanish Netherlands, seizing various territories in his wife's name; this rationalised his frontier and put him in a better position to seize and hold the remaining provinces when Carlos died. Louis's aggression was checked on this occasion by the formation of the Triple Alliance of England, the Dutch and Sweden, but he soon won Charles II over to the idea of a joint war against the Dutch. By the Secret Treaty of Dover (1670), the two Kings agreed to attack and partition the republic. Charles wanted to grab as much as possible of the Dutch trade and colonial possessions and to avenge his defeat in the war of 1665–7. Louis's motives were more complex. The Dutch had shown in 1668 that they rather than the Spaniards were the main obstacle to his conquest of the Spanish Netherlands, and Louis wanted to punish this upstart Calvinist republic for having opposed him on that occasion. His motives were also economic: Colbert wanted in particular to seize and reopen the great port of Antwerp which, he hoped, would lead to the eclipse of Amsterdam and London as commercial centres. Charles's notorious promise to declare himself a Catholic was of minimal importance: he had no intention of fulfilling it and Louis did not particularly want him to. Both were far more interested in the war.

Charles hoped to use William and his supporters to harass the States party, which he regarded as their common enemy. He saw William as his mother had done, as an Englishman and a Stuart, and expected him to follow the line of policy that his royal uncle laid down. He therefore expressed an interest in William's elevation and invited him to England. William went over late in 1670 and stayed four months. He was royally feasted by the City of London and received degrees from both universities. He was bored by the horse-racing at Newmarket and outfaced by his uncles' endless eating and drinking. They did manage to get him drunk once and he was later found trying to climb into the lodgings of the maids of honour. Charles found William reserved, plainly dressed and abstemious, and rather more 'Dutch' than he had expected, but he still thought that he would follow the 'Orange', or rather English, interest.

In 1671 and early 1672, as Louis's military preparations became apparent, events within the republic moved towards a

28

A seventeenth-century
tile showing a Dutch
sailing ship.

crisis. The Orangists and their popular supporters, egged on by
English agents, urged that William should be made captain
general so that he could use his influence with Charles to
separate England from France; this view, though widely held,
rested on complete ignorance of Charles's intentions. De Witt
and the States party resisted William's elevation because they
feared both that William was ambitious for royal power and
that he was a tool of his uncle. These fears were to prove unfounded. William himself was unaware of the extent of
Charles's commitment to France and hoped to use his uncle's
influence to help him secure the places which he felt were right-
fully his. His desire for power increased as the French menace
grew: he felt he *needed* power to defend his country, which he
believed the States party was either unable or unwilling to do.
As his need for power grew, he was ready to take great risks in
order to secure it. This can be illustrated by the offer which he
made to Charles in January 1672:

29

Unless His Majesty be too closely bound to France, he may never find a better opportunity for obtaining from the States whatever he wish and should His Majesty be willing to let me know his desires, I am confident that, so long as they are not directly hostile to the foundations of this Republic, I shall be able to obtain them for him in spite of Mr Grand Pensionary de Witt and his cabal, who will thereby be worsted while I and my friends, in whom His Majesty can place his trust, will be placed at the helm; once His Majesty has had his wish he will, moreover, be able to count on this state for all time. I have no doubt that His Majesty will believe that, so long as I have any authority in this state, I shall be utterly devoted to His Majesty's interests, in so far as my honour and the faith which I owe to this country can allow me.

William did qualify his offer of submission with an insistence that the foundations of the republic should be preserved, but he was playing a dangerous game and it was as well for him that Charles asked for more than he could give and that the letter remained secret. It shows the confusion of aspirations, fears and misconceptions from which sprang the revolution of 1672.

The deadlock between Holland and the other six provinces on the question of William's elevation paralysed the republic's preparations for war. The navy, mostly provided by Holland, was in good shape and helped save the republic in 1672–3; but the army was a shambles. William was at last made captain general for one year, but when he heard of the preparations of the great French army, he was duly pessimistic: 'To oppose to all that a captain general who has no experience and very few advisers! God must come to our aid!' Late in April 1672 Louis began his campaign. It soon became a stately progress as one garrison after another surrendered without a fight. In May de Witt ordered that the dikes should be cut, to create a last line of defence for the province of Holland. On 8 June William's little army, now only nine thousand men, withdrew behind this 'water-line'; it was still far from complete and there seemed little hope of holding it as the French overran the province of Utrecht. If Louis had attacked the water-line at once he would probably have broken through; but he did not, for two reasons: he wasted valuable time mopping up the garrisons which stood in his way, and he believed he had already done enough. He did not want to annexe the republic; he wanted

The battle of Schooneweld, June 1973. The allied French and English fleets suffered heavy losses when confronted with the augmented Dutch fleet. Contemporary Dutch engraving.

ELDINGE VANDE TWEE BLOEDIGE ZEESLAGEN, GEHOUDEN op den 7 en 14 Iuny 1673 d'Maghtige Zee vlooten van Vranckryck, en Engelandt, tegen die vande Vereenigde Nederlanden

only to inflict such a crushing defeat on the Dutch that they would no longer be able to hinder French military or commercial expansion. Convinced that the Dutch would have to accept whatever terms he imposed, he pushed his demands higher and higher. By the time the Dutch rejected them and broke off negotiations on 27 June, the water-line had grown stronger and William's little army had grown in size and determination.

If Holland was now in a better condition to resist the French, its internal situation was alarming. With each humiliation, the people's anger grew and sought scapegoats among the regents (although Orangists in the army had often showed themselves the most cowardly and defeatist). English and Orangist propaganda insisted that the kindly Charles II had made war only because the selfish regents of Holland had stubbornly refused to give William his rightful offices. It was alleged that the States party would sooner sell the republic to the French than see William as stadholder. Many believed that once William became stadholder, England would join with the Dutch against France. The States of Holland bowed to the pressure; on 24 June they made William stadholder, and the States General made him captain general for life. His powers were still mainly advisory, however, and he could still meet with obstruction and opposition. To defeat the French, William believed that he needed more effective and untrammelled power and that he had to break the opposition of the States party. To this end he pursued two distinct policies. First, he continued to try to do a deal with Charles II which would take England out of the war and strengthen his position in the republic. Secondly, he showed himself ready to exploit and even encourage popular violence against his political opponents.

His negotiations with Charles came to nothing. Charles was ready to help him secure sovereignty over the United Provinces, but his price (large territorial and commercial concessions) was too high. William was reported to have said that 'He liked better the condition of stadholder which they [the States] had given him and that he believed himself obliged in conscience and honour not to prefer his interest before his obligation.' Moreover, as events in the republic went more and more in his favour, he realised that he did not need his uncle's help.

William's reaction to the upsurge of popular violence was mixed. Like most of the rioters, he had no time for democracy and he had no wish to encourage disorder. But the riots had already assisted his elevation and they were directed against his political enemies. The temptation to exploit the disturbances further was great and William yielded to it. He did little to stop the violence or the clamour for the punishment of de Witt. He pointedly refused to declare that de Witt was innocent of the crimes with which Orangist pamphlets charged him. As a result, de Witt resigned his post as Grand Pensionary of Holland and was replaced by William's supporter Gaspar Fagel. On 5 August a letter from Charles II to William was published which blamed the States party for the war and alleged that Charles's sole aim in making war had been to secure William's just rights. William did not directly order the publication of the letter, but he had sent it to Fagel to use as he thought fit, and Fagel had had it read in the States General and the States of Holland. As one contemporary remarked, those who ordered its publication 'could have had no other intention than to bring the men at the helm into ill-repute and to expose them to popular fury'.

The publication had the desired effect. De Witt's brother Cornelis was already in prison at The Hague on a trumped-up charge. On 10 August Johan was lured to the prison by a forged letter which purported to come from his brother. Both were trapped inside and the crowd outside grew rapidly. Eventually it broke down the doors, dragged the brothers outside, murdered them and savagely mutilated their bodies. Fingers, toes and eyes were sold as souvenirs. The lynching was clearly carefully organised. Leading Orangists like Zuylestein were present. The local Reformed clergy exulted in God's vengeance on these two sinners. William himself neither directly authorised nor openly approved the murders, but he had not discouraged the popular movement and had given it a certain implicit encouragement: the publication of Charles's letter was especially provocative. Moreover, he did nothing to punish those responsible for the outrage; he told a deputy of the States of Holland, rather disingenuously, that he could not proceed with rigour as the crime had been committed by some of the leading citizens; he even gave government jobs to some of the ringleaders. William's equivocal reaction to the murders is not very attractive, but William was not squeamish and his was not a squeamish age. William was a hard man, but seventeenth-century politics was a hard and violent business: even the 'Merry Monarch', Charles II, tried hard to persuade Parliament to condemn to death his trusty old servant the Earl of Clarendon.

The de Witts' murder led directly to the removal of the last

Gaspar Fagel, whose wide experience and shrewd statesmanship fitted him well for the post of Grand Pensionary of Holland which he took over from de Witt. Through his efforts Holland came into line with Orange policies.

33

The murder of the de Witt
brothers: an engraving by
Romyn de Hooghe,
showing Cornelis (left)
and Jan (right) as insets.
Their mutilated limbs and
vitals were eagerly
bought, and their crimes
crystallised in the verse:
'Orange they stifled,
  While Britain they
    scorned.'

35

barriers to William's seizure of effective power. A week later the States of Holland authorised him to change as many of the members of the town councils as he thought fit. They were encouraged to do so by Fagel's threat that 'It was far better to forgo a mere formality than to allow the commonalty to impose order.' Less than a third of the regents of Holland were in fact dismissed and they were replaced by men of similar social standing. All William's opponents were removed or cowed, however, and in many towns the independence and civic spirit of the regents were permanently damaged. William's rise to power was now complete. He held the offices of his ancestors, which were made hereditary in 1674, and he had (for the time being) reduced the likelihood of opposition to his direction of war and diplomacy. The concentration of power in William's hands soon bore fruit: late in 1672 he began to take the offensive against France and by the end of 1673 almost all the French troops had left Dutch soil. William had, deservedly, won for himself the title of 'The Redeemer of the Fatherland'.

'The Redeemer of the Fatherland'

William's political apprenticeship was thus a hard one. Already one can see in him the mixture of authoritarianism and practicality, of integrity and unscrupulousness that he was later to show as king of England. Perhaps the key to an understanding of his character and behaviour lies in his clear-sighted distinguishing between ends and means. Once he had achieved the offices which he regarded as his birthright, he came to see power, in Holland or in England, as a means to an end, not an end in itself. From 1672 his main concern was the containment of France; he was always interested primarily in war and diplomacy, the main responsibilities of any seventeenth-century prince. There was often, however, a stark contrast between the patriotism and integrity of the motives behind his foreign policy and the sordid and unscrupulous methods which he used against his opponents at home – witness his reaction to the riots of 1672 and the murder of the de Witts. He was always passionately convinced of his own right to rule, of the purity of his intentions and of his own rightness. These convictions had their roots partly in his own personality and religious faith and partly in his upbringing. They made him very intolerant of the opinions of others if those opinions led them to obstruct what he saw as his European mission. Always a statesman rather than a politician, he had little but scorn for politicians with their wheeling and dealing, their selfish ambitions and their obsession with local and sectional interests. As a result, he treated them with the contempt and lack of scruple which he thought they deserved.

These authoritarian tendencies might have led him to aspire to become an absolute monarch: in an ideal world, that was probably what he would have wanted to be. However, the world was not ideal and William was a realist who, anyway, saw power as a means rather than as an end in itself. In order to have a free hand abroad, William was ready to compromise at home, both in Holland and in England; in domestic affairs he was prepared to delegate responsibility, to work within the existing system and to use to the full the powers that he possessed, officially or unofficially. By doing so, he left himself free to pursue the objectives which really mattered to him.

2 Marriage and Love 1672-85

IF WILLIAM COMPLETED his political apprenticeship in 1672, the next few years saw him gain experience as a soldier. He was never happier than when he was on campaign; in battle he lost his usual reserve and became 'all fire'. Sir William Temple, the English diplomat, wrote: '[He] loves the trade and thinks himself the better in health and humour the less he is at rest.' His education had given him a basic grounding in military theory and a strong sense of his responsibilities as a military leader. His religious faith reinforced his total physical courage: 'I dare to say without vanity that life will always be less dear to me than the satisfaction of living up to the expectations men have of me.' In battle he led by example. He always wore the conspicuous star of the Order of the Garter and ignored the pleas of his wife and the States General to be a little more cautious. He seemed to bear a charmed life: he was slightly wounded on numerous occasions, and at Saint Denis only the sharp shooting of his cousin Ouwerkerk saved his life.

As a general William was not in the same class as a Turenne or a Marlborough. They manœuvred with care and skill and never gave battle until they were sure that they would win; they showed similar care and patience in their sieges. William never fully mastered the intricacies of siege warfare and relied on crude, repeated and often costly assaults. He gave battle far more readily than most generals, often when conditions were not really favourable. As a result, he fought a lot of battles and lost many of them. This partly reflected his own direct and impatient temperament, but he also suffered from disadvantages which Louis XIV's marshals, in particular, did not have. First, in 1672 the Dutch army was riddled with cowardice, incompetence and indiscipline. It took William and his lieutenant and mentor, Prince von Waldeck, years of hard work and harsh punishments to lick the soldiers into shape. Secondly, William usually fought as leader of a coalition; it often proved difficult to co-ordinate the various armies. Thirdly, whereas Louis had the superb administrative machine built up by Louvois and Colbert, William ultimately depended on the States General for money and men. This meant, in effect, that he could not afford to spend the whole campaigning season in inconclusive manœuvres; he had to produce results and so had to fight, and if possible win, in order to maintain Dutch support for the war.

Sir William Temple, painted by Gaspar Netscher. He came to The Hague in 1668 as England's ambassador to the Dutch Court, and reported that William was 'a Prince of many virtues'. The admiration was mutual and William valued his friend's advice throughout the years.

Considering that he usually had armies that were inferior both in numbers and in quality to the French, it is notable that he could, on his day, achieve considerable successes. In 1674 he fought a bloody drawn battle at Seneffe against the great Condé, now admittedly past his best, and clearly impressed him: 'The Prince of Orange has acted in all respects like an old captain, except in venturing his life too much, like a young one.' Four years later William got the better of Luxembourg at Saint Denis and in 1695 he took Namur, which had been fortified by Vauban himself and which the French had regarded as impregnable. Even when he lost, moreover, William often managed to delay French advances, to disrupt their manœuvres or to limit

41

their gains. Against the great army of Louis XIV, such limited achievements were all that could usually be hoped for.

In his first years as stadholder, William also had to find his feet as a diplomat. His first concern was England. He hoped to persuade Charles to join with him against France, but he was soon disillusioned. Charles threatened to have him treated like de Witt, to which William replied: 'Do not think that I can be frightened by your threats of having me torn in pieces by the rabble; I am not fearful by nature.' Charles's intractability led William, reluctantly, to seek to undermine him by supporting the opposition within England to the Court and to the alliance with France. The war, the alliance, the Declaration of Indulgence of 1672 (which gave toleration to all religious dissenters, including Catholics), the Duke of York's conversion to Catholicism, the quartering of troops near London – all these circumstances created great anxiety in England. It was all too easy for Dutch agents and propaganda to suggest that they were all part of a great plot to impose 'Popery and arbitrary government' in England and to exterminate Protestantism in Europe. Catholicism and absolutism were the twin bugbears which most alarmed seventeenth-century Englishmen, and Charles's new ally, Louis XIV, was the champion of both. Late in 1673 Parliament was so out of control that Charles actually consulted an astrologer about the best time to recall it. Without Parliament, he had no money to continue the war. In February 1674 he made peace with the Dutch.

William was certainly behind some of the Dutch propaganda and political agitation. Although he disapproved on principle of fomenting opposition to lawful authority, he was sometimes driven by the pressing needs of war and diplomacy to act contrary to his principles. This happened in Holland in 1672 and in England in 1672–3; it was to happen again in 1688. For the present, however, he kept secret his connections with the English opposition and so avoided compromising himself in the eyes of his uncles. Meanwhile, on the Continent, he managed to secure the neutrality of Louis's other allies and built up a coalition against France whose chief members were the Dutch and the two Habsburg rulers – the King of Spain and the Holy Roman Emperor. Neither was a particularly useful ally. Spain was too weak to defend the Spanish Netherlands without

OPPOSITE A Court ball held at The Hague in 1686. The engraving is by D. Marot.

43

considerable outside help. The Emperor Leopold was more
powerful, but his main interests lay in Germany and so his prim-
ary concern was to check French aggression in the Rhineland
(in which he was largely successful). The Imperial generals were
therefore very reluctant to risk heavy casualties in the Netherlands. Most were unco-operative and one, the Count de
Souches, was more than a little dotty. He kept changing his
mind and feigned sickness in order to avoid attending councils of
war. He demanded far more men than he needed and sent off all

The signing of the Peace of Nymegen in 1678: a contemporary engraving. William failed to prevent the States General from accepting humiliating terms.

his guns and powder in the middle of a siege. Finally he marched his men straight through the Dutch infantry, causing utter chaos. Souches was recalled and William became supreme commander but he still had great difficulties in securing the full co-operation of his allies.

With the formation of the coalition against France, the pattern of the war changed. William's aim was now not to defend the republic itself but to limit French gains in the Spanish Netherlands. Louis for his part abandoned his hopes of crushing the Dutch and concentrated on rationalising his northern frontier. The war, meanwhile, placed a heavy burden on the French economy; high taxes and bad harvests provoked peasant unrest. Louis therefore became anxious for peace, and made several proposals to the Dutch. William, aware of his difficulties, hoped to make Louis disgorge all his conquests since 1659. In this he was over-optimistic. In the 1670s, as in the 1690s, Louis might have all sorts of problems at home, but his army could still go on winning; each year it captured a few more towns. Meanwhile, William too faced problems at home. If the war placed a heavy burden on France, with its population of twenty million, it placed a heavier burden on the Dutch republic, with not much more than two million. War disrupted the trade on which the Dutch depended, while England was obviously profiting from her neutrality. Once the danger to the republic's territory had been removed, the war seemed expensive and unnecessary. After the disastrous failure of William's attempt to retake Maastricht in 1676, even Fagel became convinced that the Dutch should cut their losses and make peace.

As so often, doubts in Holland about the wisdom of William's foreign policy became linked with anxiety about his ambitions at home. Fears revived that he wanted to set up as king. In 1675 he was offered the title of Duke of Gelderland, which would have given him sovereign power in that province. When Holland and Zeeland made their opposition clear, he reluctantly rejected the offer, referring angrily to those who 'did not scruple to baptise with the name of liberty and the defence of the privileges those measures taken to humiliate and oppress our person'. The opposition to William's foreign policy and domestic ambitions was led by Holland and above all by Amsterdam. The regents there had played along with William

45

in 1672–3; now, as William's popularity waned with heavy taxation and the interruption of trade, the Amsterdammers became increasingly clamorous for peace. If William was to continue the war (and, as he hoped, bring Louis to his knees), he had to make the Dutch believe that victory was possible: he had to bring more forces to the allied side. To this end, he looked once more towards England and reconsidered the possibility of marrying his cousin Mary, the elder daughter of the Duke of York.

James, Duke of York had met Mary's mother, Anne Hyde, in exile, while she was maid of honour to William's mother. In November 1659 they entered into a secret contract of marriage, which he began to regret when his brother was restored to the throne the following year. By that time, however, Anne was pregnant and James, somewhat reluctantly, made an honest woman of her. They were married secretly on 3 September 1660 and Anne gave birth to a son on 22 October. (He died in May 1661.) No one welcomed the match. Anne's father, the Lord Chancellor (later created Earl of Clarendon), was furious at his daughter's misbehaviour: he said loyally that he would rather see her as the Duke's whore than as his wife and he was even prepared to see her executed. Some of James's friends tried helpfully to extricate him from his embarrassment by claiming that they had enjoyed Anne's favours in an interesting variety of situations (which she vehemently denied). James's mother rushed over from France to prevent his scandalous misalliance with the daughter of a mere lawyer. But to no avail. The marriage was not really a success. Anne was intelligent and witty, but she was also bossy and with age she grew grotesquely fat. She died in 1671, a recent convert to Catholicism, having done her duty as a royal wife by giving birth eight times; two of the children survived, Mary and Anne. Their importance grew as it became apparent that Charles's Queen, Catherine of Braganza, was unlikely to have any children. After their father, the two girls were next in line in the succession to the throne.

Mary was born on 30 April 1662 at St James's Palace, 'at which', noted Pepys, 'I find nobody pleased'. She and Anne were brought up at St James's and at a house at Twickenham given to their parents by Clarendon. Mary was always her father's favourite. Pepys noted with disgust that James played

William Wissing's portrait of Mary as a child. At an early age she took part in Court masques.

with her 'with great pleasure ... like an ordinary private father'. She and Anne dined often at their father's table, which was unusual: most aristocratic children were firmly segregated from their parents. Mary's mother, on the other hand, had little time for her, and neither Mary nor James wasted many tears on her when she died. Two years later James, now an open Roman Catholic, remarried. His bride was Mary Beatrice d'Este, Princess of Modena; she was vivacious and strikingly beautiful

47

A landscape painted by the Dutch artist Cornelius Bega. It is now in Ham House.

and at fifteen was only four years older than Mary. As James remarked in his simple-minded way, 'I have provided you with a playfellow.' The girls soon began to play with her, and Mary, in particular, became very fond of their young stepmother.

Mary's religious education had begun before her father's conversion became known, and by the time of his remarriage she was firmly committed to the Church of England: 'Whatever happens,' she wrote, 'I hope that my sister and I will keep our fidelity to God and our religion unblemished.' After James's conversion, Charles gave his brother's daughters an establishment at Richmond House, away from the Court and

48

from their father's contagious Popery. James and Mary Beatrice saw the girls quite often, however, and do not seem to have tried to foist their religion on to them. The only real tension arose in 1676 when Charles appointed as Mary's spiritual mentor the combative and bigoted Bishop of London, Henry Compton. His first task was to persuade James to allow him to prepare Mary for confirmation; he succeeded, but not without leaving a residue of bad feeling on both sides. Religion apart, Mary's education was pretty minimal. She learned some French, but her days were spent mostly in prayers, games of cards, walks and gossip.

Her main companions were the six daughters of her governess, Lady Frances Villiers, but her greatest affection was reserved for Frances Apsley, who was nine years her senior. Lacking a mother's love, Mary's affectionate soul sought comfort and release in long passionate letters to the older girl, letters which reflected Mary's fondness for sentimental romances. She called Frances her 'husband' and described herself as 'your humble servant to kiss the ground where you go, to be your dog in a string, your fish in a net, your bird in a cage, your humble trout'. Most of the letters were ill-written and effusively sentimental. James and Mary Beatrice were shocked when they found out about them, but they were really only the outpourings of a warm and loving adolescent, seeking an outlet for her emotions within an all-female environment. The love that Mary now lavished on the rather embarrassed Frances was later to find a more acceptable, and eventually more responsive, recipient in William.

The first rumours that William might marry Mary came when he visited England in 1670. Four years later Charles revived the idea, but William replied: 'I cannot leave the battle-field, nor believe that it would be agreeable for a lady to be where the battlefield is.' By 1676 the war was going badly, William's position in the republic was deteriorating and he began to consider asking for Mary's hand. Although Mary was the next heir to the throne after her father, in many ways the prospect of marrying her was not very attractive. Her father was unlikely to offer much of a dowry but William, always a careful manager, did not really need money. Marriage to another Mary Stuart was unlikely to be popular in Holland,

LEFT Prince William III as
a boy: the painting is by
Abraham Ragueneau. His
unsettled upbringing
made him petulant, and he
suffered from asthma.

ABOVE The *Prince's Birthday*,
by the Dutch artist Jan
Steen (1626–79), who painted
many humorous scenes
from peasant and middle-
class life in Holland.

where William's mother was remembered with little affection. William himself had nothing but contempt for the low birth of Mary's mother, who had, after all, been one of his mother's servants; he had even wondered whether the mother's lowly status might prejudice the daughter's claim to the throne. Moreover, at the time when William came to England to ask for Mary's hand, Mary Beatrice was pregnant. She gave birth to a son a few days after William's marriage to Mary; the child died soon after, but the mother was still only nineteen and was likely to have other children. (She gave birth to a son in 1688 and a daughter in 1692.) By marrying Mary, therefore, William improved his chances of succeeding to the English throne, but it was likely to be some time before he succeeded and it was by no means certain that he would ever do so. The only immediate benefit he could hope for was a somewhat hypothetical one: he hoped that the marriage would give him enough extra influence with Charles to enable him to bring England in to the alliance against France. Although this policy had the support of some of Charles's ministers, notably Danby, it was to prove a failure.

If William's motives were mainly diplomatic, he was not indifferent to the personality of his prospective bride. In 1676 he asked Temple for an account of her character: 'If he should meet with one to give him trouble at home, it was what he should not be able to bear, who was like to have enough abroad in the course of his life.' In October 1677 he came over to England and made every effort to play the courtier to Charles and his brother. Charles, however, wanted to discuss terms for a peace (which France wanted) before considering his niece's marriage. William threatened to return home unless his request for Mary's hand was answered. After a delay, Charles agreed. James, he said, would do as he was told: 'God's fish, he must consent.' He did, but reluctantly; and when Mary was told of her fate, she wept for a day and a half.

It was not surprising that she found William unattractive. She was fifteen, tall (five feet eleven) and handsome, dressed in the latest Court fashions. He was almost twenty-seven, and over four inches shorter. He wore his own hair rather than a wig and was dressed mostly in black, as was the Dutch custom: 'The plainest man ever seen and of no fashion at all,' remarked one

'God's fish, he must consent'

lady. As Burnet described him later, he was hardly love's young dream:

> He had a thin and weak body, was brown haired and of a clear and delicate constitution: he had a Roman eagle nose, bright and sparkling eyes, a large front [forehead] and a countenance composed to gravity and authority. ... His behaviour was solemn and serious, seldom cheerful and but with a few: he spoke little and very slowly and most commonly with a disgusting dryness.

He had forgotten most of his English and found breathing even more difficult than usual in the claustrophobic atmosphere of Whitehall. Not surprisingly, the wedding, which took place on 4 November (William's birthday), was not a jolly affair. At William's request the ceremony was small and private. Anne and Lady Frances Villiers had smallpox and so could not come. William, as usual, looked solemn, James looked gloomy and Mary was in tears. Only the King was cheerful, if hardly tactful: 'Come bishop!', he told Compton, 'Make all the haste you can, lest my sister the Duchess of York should bring us a boy and then the marriage would be disappointed.' Afterwards the couple were put to bed, where they received the congratulations of the Court. Then Charles himself drew the curtains round the bed, saying 'Now nephew, to your work! Hey! St George for England!'

The marriage was very popular in England; it seemed to show that England was escaping at last from its subordination to France. The rejoicings in London formed a sharp contrast to the gloom of the newly-married couple. William had not got the alliance against France that he wanted and, indeed, his marriage seemed to have given him no more influence with his uncle. Mary Beatrice gave birth to a son, and William was obliged to stand as his godfather. The States General were clearly less than delighted about the marriage, although they gave their consent. The dowry was small, just enough to pay for the jewels which William had given Mary as a wedding present. William found the confusion and superficiality of Charles's Court increasingly irritating and there were matters back in Holland which called for his attention: small wonder that he was impatient to go home. Mary, on the other hand, dreaded going. When the Queen told her that she too had had to travel

A painting of parrots by James Bogdani. Bogdani was a Hungarian who studied painting in Vienna and settled in England. Here he became Court painter to William and Mary.

to a strange land, she replied: 'Madam, you came into England; I am going out of England.' The wind was unfavourable and their departure was delayed until the 19th. Mary and her step-mother wept copiously; she was unable to bid farewell to Anne, who still had smallpox. In the Thames estuary the wind turned against them. William, unable to face another tearful farewell, refused to return to London so they waited at Canterbury. They finally sailed on the 27th. It was a dreadful crossing. Everyone except Mary was sick. When they eventually landed, the roads were impassable so they had to walk three miles before their coaches could pick them up. Their married life had not had an auspicious beginning.

The first two years of marriage were difficult for both of them. William was at first preoccupied with the war. In 1678 Louis xiv at last scared the Dutch into making peace by taking Ghent and Ypres. William was furious – Charles ii had actually been persuaded to enter the war – but there was nothing he could do. Mary feared for his safety while he was on campaign: 'What can be more cruel in the world than parting with what one loves and not only common parting but parting so as may be never to meet again.' She also had troubles of her own. Early

54

in 1678 she became pregnant, but miscarried after a long and bumpy coach journey to meet William at Breda. Later that year she believed she was pregnant again and her doctors confirmed it. She started to furnish a nursery, and William asked the States General to stand as sponsors for the child. But nine months came and went and it became apparent that there would be no baby. It is possible that her miscarriage had caused permanent damage; her health was certainly bad during the following year and she never conceived again. On top of this, William was touchy and irritable after his failure to prevent the peace and offered her little comfort. He had a series of quarrels with Mary's ladies in waiting, a silly gossipy bunch – the 'beggarly bitches', one contemporary called them. He was also annoyed by the fussing of Mary's chaplains, who feared that her pure Anglicanism might be tainted by her husband's Calvinism. Finally, events in England had taken an ugly turn. Titus Oates's revelations of an alleged Popish Plot led to a growing pressure that James should be excluded from the succession to the throne, on the grounds that he was a Catholic. Charles packed his brother off to Brussels, whence he came to visit his son-in-law and lectured him endlessly on the perils confronting the monarchy.

Gradually, however, their relationship improved. William and Mary had in common a firm religious faith and high standards of personal conduct. Mary soon came to realise that her place in William's life would be a limited one. William regarded politics and diplomacy as man's work. Mary was not keen on hunting (she was a poor horsewoman) and anyway William also saw hunting as a male preserve. He always preferred the easy male camaraderie of the camp and the hunting field to the formality of the Court. He had a few close friends, with whom he spent much of his time: his cousins Odijk and Ouwerkerk and, above all, Bentinck, who had slept in William's bed to draw off the fever when he had smallpox in 1675 and who later married Anne Villiers, one of Mary's ladies. From time to time William was attracted to handsome young men but he was never actively homosexual; being a shy man, he preferred the company of men whom he knew well to that of women. He does not seem to have been highly sexed and there are few stories of any youthful indiscretions with women. Even his famous affair with Elizabeth Villiers was more cerebral than physical.

In this intensely active male world of William's, there was still a place for Mary and she filled it. She was a warm, loving person and soon concentrated her affection on her husband. He for his part gradually thawed; he became relaxed, affable and (much later) loving. She was careful never to talk business with him: 'I saw him so full of it that I thought, and he has told me so himself, that when he could get away from it he was glad to come to me and have his thoughts diverted by other discourse.' Mary also served as a hostess and 'first lady' of such unimpeachable rectitude that even the Reformed clergy could find little fault with her, apart from a fondness for petty gambling and for occasional visits to the theatre. She soon became as popular as her husband and, rather to her surprise, she fell in love with the Dutch people and countryside. She liked the politeness, seriousness and piety which gave the Dutch a dignity that was free from pomp or affectation. Here she found little of the hypocrisy, sycophancy and backbiting of Charles II's Court. She also liked the Dutch houses, which were airy, well-proportioned and spotlessly clean – a great change from Whitehall, with its endless jumble of corridors and apartments, its smoke, dirt, stench and confusion. While refuse and sewage often lay in the streets in England, the Dutch burghers spent much time and money cleansing and beautifying their towns which, needless to say, made them much pleasanter to walk in.

Mary soon came to share with the Dutch and with William an interest in domestic architecture, interior decoration and gardens. She had ample scope in the various Orange palaces, some of them seldom used. The stadholder's official residence, which he shared with the States General, was the Binnenhof at The Hague, but both William and Mary preferred their country houses. Mary's favourite was Honselaersdijk, only seven miles from The Hague, which had forests at the rear and dunes and the sea at the front. Built by Frederick Henry, it was widely regarded as the finest house in the United Provinces and contained some of William's finest pictures. The other houses were smaller – the House in the Wood, Soestdijk and Dieren; each was improved and the two last had formal gardens added. William particularly liked Dieren. The hunting in the forests of

'*He was glad to come to me and have his thoughts diverted*'

56

Gelderland was excellent, the air was fresh and the house was so small that he had to leave most of the Court behind, so he could hand-pick his company. In 1686 William began to build a great new palace at Het Loo, near Dieren, with superb formal gardens in the French style. If it was not intended to be the Dutch answer to Versailles, it was still impressive. The work took nine years to complete and Mary was not to see it finished.

Mary's time in Holland passed pleasantly enough. She spent her days in walks, in boat-trips on the canals, in sewing, cards or gossip with her ladies. She and William usually dined separately, each with their own household. Their pleasures were of a domestic, family kind – card-games and tea or supper parties with the Bentincks and other close friends and occasional visitors. As a Court, theirs was homely, relaxed and orderly, very different from the rough and tumble of Whitehall or the stultifying formality of Versailles. In this atmosphere, the couple whose marriage had been one of diplomatic convenience gradually grew to respect and love one another, in spite of the political difficulties of the early years of their marriage.

Louis XIV did not take long to resume his aggression. He refused to pay William the revenues from those of his estates which were in French hands. More seriously, French troops overran and looted Orange and began to persecute the Protestants there. This act of vindictiveness hardened William's dislike for Louis into an undying hatred. (He was never anti-French as such: he bought a wide variety of goods in France and imported French architects and landscape gardeners for his palaces.) In the years after 1678 Louis also undertook a series of localised acts of aggression, under the pretext of recovering French 'rights' over particular towns and territories. Most of these were in the Rhineland, where the local princes were too weak to resist, while their nominal overlord, the Emperor, was preoccupied with defence against the Turks. More seriously, from the Dutch point of view, Louis tried to seize Luxembourg, which belonged to Spain. William tried desperately to persuade the English and Dutch to resist the French King. But Charles had relapsed into neutrality thanks to a French pension, and the States General did not think the time was right for a new war with France. They realised that if Louis resumed his encroachments on the Spanish Netherlands, the Dutch would eventually

The Homes of the Princes of Orange

Both William and Mary were enthusiastic about the decoration and improvement of their homes and the landscaping and cultivation of the various palace gardens. Here are three of the palaces they used most.

BELOW The delightful House in the Wood on the outskirts of The Hague. This engraving by A. Beek shows the approach to the house.

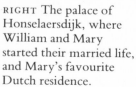
RIGHT The palace of Honselaersdijk, where William and Mary started their married life, and Mary's favourite Dutch residence.

LEFT De Hooghe's engraving of the palace of Het Loo, showing the beautiful formal gardens laid out on the French pattern.

Delft tiles:

ABOVE A tile based on a
design by D. Marot,
c. 1694.
RIGHT A design
incorporating oriental
flowers and birds, c. 1700.

have to fight. But the Rhineland was far away and Louis was richer than they were.

The States General regarded as irresponsible William's call for war each time Louis embarked on another act of aggression: William did not have to foot the bill. William regarded the States General and especially the men of Amsterdam as pusillanimous and unpatriotic, putting their own profits before the security of Europe; he pointed out that some leading Amsterdam politicians were in cahoots with d'Avaux, the French ambassador. But despite all his threats and entreaties, William was unable to get his way. When Spain, in desperation, declared war in 1683 no one came to her aid. Louis graciously agreed to a twenty years' truce in 1684, whereby he kept all his ill-gotten gains, including Luxembourg and the key city of Strasbourg. By his policy of intense but piecemeal aggression, Louis had strengthened and extended his frontiers without provoking a major coalition against him. The success of this policy led him to try it again in 1688, with disastrous results.

Meanwhile, what of England? William had been embarrassed by the pressure to exclude his father-in-law from the throne. He was less worried by the prospect of James's exclusion (which, he thought, would fall of itself, as Parliament was not competent to do it) than by Charles's proposals of limitations on the powers of a future Catholic king: he feared that these might also weaken James's Protestant heirs. Some of the wilder Exclusionists (or Whigs, as they became known) wanted Charles's bastard son, the Duke of Monmouth, to succeed instead of James, but William believed, rightly, that he had little to fear from him. Most of the Whigs supported Mary's claim rather than Monmouth's; Monmouth himself had good looks, charm and charisma, but precious little else: he lacked the ability to be dangerous. William therefore sat tight and refused to intervene. Events were to vindicate his judgment. The clamour for exclusion proved to contain more noise than substance. The King and the House of Lords held firm and in November 1680 the Exclusion Bill was rejected.

At this point William made a serious error of judgment. He had assumed that Charles would graciously accept the Bill and then take steps to ensure that it would never be implemented. William feared that his firm stand would lead to a major crisis

or even civil war, which would put England out of European
affairs for some time. Fagel and Henry Sidney (the English
ambassador at The Hague and a close friend of William's)
drew up a memorial from the States General which urged
Charles to come to terms with Parliament. William himself
warned Charles of the dangers of offering to limit the prerogative. Both Charles and James were annoyed at these
attempts to interfere in English affairs, and William's relations

with his uncles reached rock bottom when he visited England in July 1681. He had hoped to persuade Charles to call Parliament and so raise money for a war against France. He soon realised that he was wrong. Charles had no intention of calling Parliament and the Whigs were obsessed with exclusion and totally uninterested in what happened abroad. Charles showed his annoyance at William's contacts with the Whigs. Twice William was invited to dine in that stronghold of Whiggery, the City of London; twice Charles ordered him to come to Windsor, so that he could not go. When William asked permission to visit England in 1683, it was refused. William continued to provoke his uncles' wrath: in the winter of 1684–5, when Monmouth was in disgrace, William received him warmly and gave him full military honours. Mary danced frequently with her charming young cousin and tucked up her skirts and went skating with him. It was even rumoured that they had all gone to a comedy on 30 January, the holiest day in the Stuart calendar, the anniversary of Charles I's execution. Then, amid all the gaiety, came the news that Charles had died on 6 February, and that his brother had been proclaimed as King James II.

3
The Catholic King
1685-8

WITH JAMES'S ACCESSION, Mary became heiress presumptive to the English throne. Her greater dignity was symbolised by a growing formality at her Court, where her pages now knelt to serve her. Moreover, the chances of her succeeding her father seemed much greater now than at the time of her marriage. All Mary Beatrice's children had died young and she had not been pregnant since 1682. It seemed unlikely that she would provide James with the son who would take precedence in the succession over the daughters of the first marriage. James was now fifty-one. It seemed just a matter of time before his death would enable William to gain control of the resources of England and to bring them into the struggle against France. For much of James's reign, therefore, William simply watched and waited; his main concern was to see that nothing happened that would jeopardise his and Mary's rights.

When James II came to the throne, the power of the Stuart monarchy was at its zenith. This may seem rather surprising after Parliament had fought, defeated and executed Charles I, but the impact of these events on seventeenth-century Englishmen was ambivalent. The 'revolution' of 1640–60 had certainly seen the emergence of new and radical political ideas and there were some who embraced them wholeheartedly. But most of the nobles and gentlemen who governed the shires and sat in Parliament were and remained intensely conservative. They had resisted Charles I's innovations precisely because they were innovations and they were genuinely surprised and disconcerted when their resistance led to civil war. Their alarm turned to horror with the execution of the King, the establishment of military rule, the smashing of the old ecclesiastical order and the apparently imminent destruction of the traditional social order. The ruling elite, the 'political nation', greeted the restoration of the monarchy with a collective sigh of relief: it offered a chance to return to constitutional normality. Bad as the Stuarts might be, the men of property had experienced the alternative and they had found it much, much worse. The Church of England, restored along with the monarchy, placed increasing stress on the impiety of resistance and the duty of passive obedience to lawfully-constituted authority. Many laymen, too, saw a strong monarchy as the surest safeguard against the horrors of another civil war. There was, therefore, a real

68

potential for a strong, if firmly Anglican, monarchy in the years after the Restoration.

If this potential was to be realised, the Crown had to retain and exploit the support of its natural supporters, the 'Church and King' men, the old Cavaliers, the Tories. The support of these men for the Crown was not unconditional. They expected the King to respect the constitution and govern according to law. Also their assumption that the interests of Church and King were identical presupposed that the King would support the Protestant interest abroad and that he would maintain and protect the Church at home, by persecuting Roman Catholics and Protestant Dissenters. This the later Stuarts failed to do. Charles II pursued a pro-French foreign policy and tried to give toleration to Catholics and Dissenters. James II went very much further.

In 1685, however, James's position was extremely strong. The old Cavaliers' earlier dissatisfaction with Charles's behaviour had been forgotten during the Exclusion Crisis; the Whigs' rather phoney radicalism had revived the Tories' fears of civil war – ''41 is here again', was the cry. The Tories rallied to the Crown and received their reward, in the form of a monopoly of offices, the prosecution of leading Whigs and the persecution of Dissenters. The elections of 1679–81 had shown the strength of the Whigs' hold on the Parliamentary boroughs. The Crown and the Tories set out to break that hold. The law courts found legal pretexts to confiscate the boroughs' charters; new charters were then issued which gave the Crown sweeping powers to reduce the electorate and to control appointments to municipal offices. The Crown accordingly used these powers to put in its Tory allies and their dependents. The elections of 1685 showed how successful this process had been. A solidly Tory House of Commons was elected; there were only about forty MPs whom James did not regard as 'safe'. Parliament duly voted James an ample revenue, sufficient to enable him to keep up an army of nearly twenty thousand men. In 1685, then, James did what no other Stuart king had done or tried to do; with the help of the Tories he had successfully run a general election and secured the election of the men he wanted; in doing so he had gone a long way towards taming Parliament.

This spectacular success throws into even sharper relief the

Anne Hyde, Duchess of York, in 1670: the portrait is after Lely. James had first met her at Breda, where she was lady-in-waiting to Mary Stuart, mother of William of Orange. Anne soon realised that her marriage would not put a stop to James's infidelities, and, according to Grammont, consoled herself by becoming 'one of the highest feeders in England'.

magnitude of James's subsequent failure. Single-handed, he succeeded in turning back the tide of history. In the later seventeenth century the trend throughout Europe was towards stronger, more centralised monarchy. (Even in the Dutch republic, William's offices had been made hereditary.) England's central administration was tiny compared with that of, say, France, and the English Parliament was an unusually assertive and obstreperous representative body. Even so, in the early 1680s the English monarchy made hesitant steps towards centralisation and much more effective steps towards bringing Parliament to heel. But the movement towards stronger monarchy depended on the Crown's keeping the co-operation of the Tories. This James failed to do because of his obsessive pursuit of the mirage of a Catholic England. With the zeal of the convert, James assumed that others would be equally convinced of the truth of Catholicism, if they were allowed to be. As he saw it, the main obstacle to their conversion lay not in the attractions of Protestantism (which he dismissed as being beneath consideration) but in fear and self-interest: fear of the penal laws, which punished all aspects of Catholic behaviour, and self-interest because the Test Acts excluded Catholics from Parliament and from all public offices. He never considered forcing people to become Catholics because he lacked the power to do so – his army was far too small for the purpose and anyway it was predominantly Protestant. His whole political strategy rested on the naïve and unfounded assumption that if only the penal laws and Test Acts could be repealed, converts to Catholicism would come forward in droves; with luck, by the time Mary succeeded him, English Catholicism would be very much stronger, perhaps even the religion of the majority.

To understand the reaction which this policy aroused, one must try to grasp the attitude of seventeenth-century Englishmen towards Catholicism. 'Popery' itself was seen as a monstrous concoction of impieties and superstitions, cooked up by priests and popes to advance their own power and profit. The Protestant version of recent English history taught that Papists had persecuted Protestants savagely under Mary and had engaged in treason against the Protestant state under Elizabeth. The identification of Charles I's Court with Popery had helped both to precipitate the civil war and to associate Catholicism with 'arbitrary government'; this association found new relevance in the 1680s as the greatest absolute ruler of all, Louis XIV, gradually intensified the persecution of his Protestant subjects. Catholicism was therefore regarded as impious, un-English and inextricably bound up with despotism and persecution. Small wonder then that James II's subjects, while they might consider repealing the penal laws, were dead set against repealing the Test Acts: Catholics, they believed, had to be kept out of positions of power.

By insisting on his Catholicising policy James alienated the Tories, his natural supporters, and so rendered unusable the most compliant Parliament of the century. But if the penal laws were to be repealed with any show of legality, James would have to have them repealed by a Parliament. Catholics were by law excluded from Parliament, so if the Anglican Tories would not co-operate, James had to seek the support of the other major religious group, the Protestant Dissenters. Hitherto James had been interested in toleration for Catholics only and had allowed the persecution of Dissenters to continue; now he set himself up as the champion of toleration for all denominations. In April 1687 he issued his Declaration of Indulgence, which suspended the penal laws and Test Acts, pending their repeal by Parliament. This was intended both to encourage conversions to Catholicism and to win over the Dissenters, without whose help that repeal could not be achieved. James's main aim now was to secure, by hook or by crook, a Parliament that would do as he wished on this one crucial issue. To this end he used the powers which the Crown had acquired over the Parliamentary boroughs to put out the Tories who had been installed in 1681–5 and to put in Dissenters. He tried to persuade both Parliamentary candidates and leading nobles and gentry to pledge themselves to support the repeal. He mounted an intensive campaign of canvassing and propaganda, using men who had learned their trade under the Exclusionist Whigs. And, when all else failed, he fell back on trickery and intimidation.

It must be stressed that James's policies were in every way more radical than those pursued by his father in the 1630s. Charles I had wanted to impose Arminianism; James wanted to promote Catholicism. Charles had exploited legal technicalities to raise money; James claimed that in ecclesiastical matters he possessed the power to suspend penal laws and pardon those who broke them: this raised fears that the King's powers might be extended to allow him to suspend all the laws of England. Charles had tried to supervise more closely the workings of local government; James made wholesale changes in the commissions of the peace and the militia which amounted to a frontal attack on what the Tory gentry regarded as their God-given right to rule the localities: in other words, by bringing in new men, often of obscure origins, to rule the shires, James flouted the traditional limitation of major local offices to a small circle of the wealthiest landowners of each county. (In doing so, incidentally, he raised unpleasant echoes of events during the Interregnum.) Finally Charles I had simply failed to

summon Parliament; James tried to control all elections and to get candidates to promise to support a particular line of policy; by doing so he threatened to turn Parliament into a mere rubber stamp for his policies.

As even the cautious and legalistic Charles I was accused of trying to establish absolutism, it is hardly surprising that the same accusation has been levelled against the far more reckless and radical James II. This is the more inevitable because both James's contemporaries and later Protestant historians assumed

ABOVE RIGHT James Scott, Duke of Monmouth, favourite illegitimate son of Charles II: an engraving from Riley's painting. Ailesbury described him as 'most charming both as to his person and engaging behaviour, a fine courtier, but of a poor understanding as to

cabinets and politics, and given wholly up to flatterers and knaves by consequence'.

ABOVE LEFT The end of the road for Monmouth's ill-timed rebellion: a Dutch print shows the ignominious defeat of Monmouth at Sedgemoor in July 1685.

that Catholicism and absolutism were inseparable, an assumption which seemed to be confirmed by the example of Louis XIV. However, it is unlikely that James's main aim was to introduce absolutism, for two reasons. First, all James's illegal and unconstitutional actions were means to an end rather than an end in themselves. They were all intended either to allow freedom of worship and employment to Catholics, or to prepare the way for a Parliament that would repeal the penal laws and Test Acts. Unlike Charles I, James never bent the law in order to

75

raise money except in the first weeks of his reign, before Parliament met; once Parliament had met there was no further need to do so. Secondly, James had no Catholic heir. There was no reason why James, already an elderly man, should try to establish an absolute monarchy for the benefit of William and Mary. Some of his Catholic courtiers did suggest that he should alter the succession in favour of a Catholic, but there is no evidence that James seriously considered doing so; indeed, James's policies were usually suffused with a sense of urgency precisely because he accepted the inevitability of the Protestant succession. But if James had no incentive to establish absolutism, as a sincere convert who wanted 'to shine in a red letter after he is dead', there was every reason why he should try to improve the position of the English Catholics.

If James's subjects misunderstood his intentions, they were thoroughly alarmed by his methods and feared the worst. Traditional attitudes to Catholicism and Catholics created an automatic distrust of the words and deeds of a Catholic king. To make matters worse, while James was arguing the merits of religious toleration, Louis xiv was trying to dragoon the Huguenots into embracing Catholicism. It was widely (but erroneously) assumed that James was both the tool and the imitator of the French King, and Louis did nothing to dispel that impression. However unconstitutional and dangerous James's measures were, they were made to seem very much worse by the misunderstandings, exaggerated fears and pure fantasies of his subjects and by the malicious propaganda of his enemies.

It is against this background that one must view William's relations with the man who was both his uncle and his father-in-law. William's attitude differed from that of most Englishmen. His prime concern was always to safeguard his and Mary's position as heirs presumptive. He was not very interested in England's affairs; to him England was important mainly as a possible member of a future coalition against France. He probably had little fear that James would succeed in establishing Catholicism. He certainly had no objection to James's strengthening the monarchy, from which William could only benefit. He really had two reasons for anxiety. First, there was a chance that something might happen to prejudice his and Mary's right to the succession. There were rumours that Anne might turn Catholic and that she or another Papist might usurp Mary's place in the succession. From the end of 1687 there was also the possibility that James's Queen might have (or pretend to have) a son. Secondly, William feared that James's behaviour might provoke a rebellion, which might in turn lead to a protracted civil war and even to the establishment of a republic. This fear was quite unfounded. Like most continentals, William had a greatly exaggerated impression of the strength of republicanism in England. In fact English republicanism had always been weak; it was originally merely the rationalisation after the event of Charles I's execution and by 1685 the republicans were no more than a pathetic remnant of the 'Good Old Cause'. Moreover, rebellion was highly unlikely. On one hand, James had a large and comparatively well-drilled standing army. On the other hand, the English nobility and gentry had long since lost both the taste and the aptitude for war. Unlike their Scottish counterparts, the English aristocracy had not rebelled against Charles I in the 1630s. Even in 1642, most hardly considered fighting until the King forced them to by making war on Parliament. Habits of obedience to lawful authority were deeply engrained; they were reinforced by the harsh punishments meted out to unsuccessful rebels: the example of Monmouth's followers was still fresh in men's minds in 1688. The northern aristocracy rose against James only when William's army was well established in the south-west, and the north was denuded of royal troops. Without William's invasion, there could have been no major rising and no Revolution in 1688.

In 1685 William set out to repair the damage done to his relations with James since 1680, but an undercurrent of suspicion and niggling hostility still remained. When he heard of Charles's death, William sent Monmouth away from his Court and even (at James's request) made vague noises of goodwill towards France. James, on the other hand, refused to pay Mary an allowance, although he paid a generous one to Anne and her gormless husband, Prince George of Denmark. (Charles II once said of George 'I have tried him drunk and I have tried him sober, and drunk or sober there is nothing in him'.) James also refused to accord William the title of 'His Royal Highness', but he did make representations to Louis XIV on behalf of William's

'Drunk or sober there is nothing in him'

77

rights in Orange. Faced with a blank refusal, he wrote to Mary that 'he could do no more in that matter unless he should declare war upon it, which he did not think fit for a thing of such small importance'. This was realistic, if not very tactful; Mary later chose to interpret it as an indication that James 'preferred to join with the King of France against my husband'. James's suspicions were increased when Monmouth managed to equip his little invasion force at Amsterdam and to sail for England unmolested. In fact William had little power in Amsterdam and, but for the bungling of James's ambassador, the ships might have been stopped. James was somewhat mollified when William sent over the English regiments in the Dutch service to

help suppress the rebellion. William in fact had little sympathy with the rebellion; he disliked rebels on principle and he had no wish to see Monmouth seize the English throne.

Despite the friction, James continued to correspond regularly with both William and Mary; he had a strong sense of the bonds of kinship and he respected Mary's position as his heir presumptive. This in itself could lead to problems. In November 1686 James sent over William Penn, the Quaker, to try to persuade William and Mary to promise to support his campaign for the repeal of the penal laws and Test Acts. However they would promise only that they would not enforce the penal laws, and they declared that they were firmly against repealing either the penal laws or the Test Acts. James continued to exhort them to change their minds and even tried to convince Mary of the merits of Catholicism. Eventually, in January 1688, William and Mary's opposition to repeal was publicly stated in *A Letter Written by Mijn Heer Fagel ... to Mr James Stewart*, many copies of which were distributed in England. Here, as so often, William stated his position and intervened in English affairs indirectly, through an official of the republic.

While James tried to persuade William and Mary to commit themselves to repeal, friction grew up on other issues. James was especially annoyed that a number of extreme Whigs and republicans had found a safe refuge in the Dutch republic. William had little time for most of them, but insisted that it was up to the various towns or the States General to order their expulsion. One refugee particularly obnoxious to James did find a welcome at William's Court: Gilbert Burnet, the Scottish divine, who was already well known for his *History of the Reformation*. He had been forced to leave England after an offensively anti-Catholic sermon in 1684 and arrived at The Hague in 1686. There his importance was twofold. First, as a propagandist: he translated Fagel's *Letter* into English and published many pamphlets attacking James's policies on religious and constitutional grounds. Secondly, Burnet indoctrinated Mary with his own Whiggish interpretation of events since the Restoration and helped her to clarify her position in relation to both her husband and her father. Mary and William had never really discussed what William's position would be when she became Queen. Mary had always assumed that he

OPPOSITE The famous *Zoological Garden of William III,* painted by M. d'Hondecoeter. William was fond of this canvas, which was hung over the fireplace in his suite at Het Loo palace.

80

would be at least co-ruler, but Burnet assured her that he would in law be no more than her consort. She was horrified at this and, encouraged by Burnet, she went to William and

> ... in a very frank manner told him that she did not know that the laws of England were so contrary to the laws of God. ... She did not think that the husband was ever to be obedient to the wife; she promised him that he should always bear rule and she asked only that he would obey the command of 'Husbands love your wives' as she should do that 'Wives be obedient to your husbands in all things.'

Bishop Burnet: portrait by Riley. The Bishop of Salisbury, author of the *History of my own Time*, proved a loyal supporter and adviser of William and Mary, often encouraging Mary to discuss difficult issues with her husband.

This touching scene completed the reconciliation of husband and wife after the protracted coolness caused by Mary's discovery of William's adultery with Elizabeth Villiers, one of her maids of honour. William was clearly attracted more by 'Betty's' wit and intelligence than by her beauty: 'the good lady squints like a dragon', wrote Swift years later. After a tip-off from three members of her household, Mary kept watch and caught William emerging from the maids' lodgings at two in the morning. He was furious both at her spying on him and at her servants' telling James what was going on. (James, perhaps realising that his own private life left much to be desired, refused to interfere.) It took some time for the unpleasantness of the incident to be forgotten.

It has sometimes been alleged that William's plan to dethrone James dated back to the start of James's reign or even to 1679, but this is incorrect. So long as nothing untoward happened, William and Mary were bound to succeed to the throne. Direct intervention in England was a possibility to be borne in mind, but the need would arise only if the situation changed radically. In the first two years of James's reign William limited himself to maintaining and extending his correspondence with English politicians of all shades of opinion. His direct intervention was limited to attempts (mostly unsuccessful) to influence James's foreign policy on particular issues. In September 1686 the Whig Lord Mordaunt urged William to invade England at once and assured him that there would be no opposition; William answered that he would be prepared to act if James tried to alter the succession or threatened the nation's religion. He privately thought Mordaunt's suggestion 'too romantical to build upon'.

There was, however, a limit to the amount he could learn from letters, especially as they were liable to be opened at the post office. In February 1687, therefore, he sent over his close friend Dijkvelt on a mission which lasted over two months. Dijkvelt's ostensible task was to give James general assurances of William's goodwill, but his real job was to sound out leading politicians, to urge them to stand firm against James's Catholicising policies and to assure them that William was determined to maintain the penal laws and Test Acts. Confined to his lodgings by a bad foot, Dijkvelt was visited by many leading figures; some also sent letters to William, including John Churchill, who assured him that both he and Princess Anne were loyal to the Protestant religion. This was important, as there had been several rumours that Anne had turned Catholic; in fact, James never really tried to convert her, although she always feared that he might set his priests on her at any time.

In August 1687, as the campaign to pack Parliament started, William sent over another special agent, Zuylestein, the son of his old tutor. Like Dijkvelt, Zuylestein was a close friend of William's who hid great political skill behind a façade of conviviality. The purpose of his mission was active rather than exploratory. He was to build up an intelligence network, to provide William with really accurate confidential information. Much of this information was passed on by a Scot, James Johnstone, whose correspondence with Bentinck still survives, with the secret material in invisible ink. Zuylestein's second task was to arrange to sound out leading Englishmen, especially army and naval officers, and to win them over to William's cause. William's chief agent in this was his old friend Henry Sidney, the former ambassador at The Hague. Clearly, William was now considering the possibility of invasion more seriously than he had the previous year, but he was still not fully committed. Zuylestein's mission opened up sources of information and enabled William to secure promises of support which he could use if and when he decided on a descent on England.

Late in 1687 it was announced that Mary Beatrice was pregnant. The joy of James's Catholic courtiers knew no bounds, but Protestants were alarmed: if she had a healthy son, he would be raised as a Catholic and there would be a Catholic dynasty.

Betty Villiers captivated William with her attractive personality and amusing conversation. Their relationship continued for many years until, after the death of Mary, she married Lord George Hamilton.

The Catholics' excessive confidence that the baby would be a boy made Protestants suspect that, even if the Queen did not have a son, her priests would get hold of a baby boy and pass him off as hers. Mary fully shared these suspicions; she wrote in April 1688: 'I have received an account of the Queen's pregnancy which gives me good cause to suspect that there is some trickery afoot. I do not know what will happen but as always I place my trust in God; it is His cause and He will take care of His Church.' She repeatedly asked Anne for details of their stepmother's condition and increased the frequency and intensity of her devotions. As she became convinced that James meant to trick her out of her inheritance and to destroy the Church that she loved, so, fortified by her prayers, she came to accept the need to dethrone him.

William did not make up his mind to invade England until the end of April 1688. The possibility that the Queen might have a son, real or bogus, probably weighed less heavily with him than the fear that the increasing intensity of James's campaign to pack Parliament might goad his subjects to rebel. Late in April William was visited at Het Loo by Arthur Herbert and William and Edward Russell. According to Burnet, William told them 'that if he was invited by some men of the best interest, and the most valued in their nation, who should both in their own name, and in the name of others who trusted them, invite him to come and rescue the nation and the religion, he believed he could be ready by the end of September to come over'.

Events in England soon confirmed his decision. On 10 June the Queen gave birth to a healthy son, which served merely to confirm the suspicions of the English Protestants and of Mary and Anne. Anne could find little real evidence that a fraud had taken place but she and Mary found little difficulty in convincing themselves that their stepbrother was spurious. William and Mary at first ordered that prayers should be said in their chapel for the Prince of Wales, but these were soon stopped. James's ambassador at The Hague threw a great party to celebrate the birth, but hardly anyone came. Soon afterwards, Zuylestein was sent to England again, ostensibly to congratulate the King and Queen but really to finalise the plans for an invasion.

OPPOSITE A cameo of William as King of England, and his Queen, by Peter Hoadley. Both saw the birth of the Prince of Wales as a fraud designed to trick them out of their inheritance.

An engraving after Kneller's portrait of
Mary of Modena, the beautiful young
second wife of James II. The birth of her child
was awaited eagerly by the Catholics but
with some apprehension by the Protestants.

86

The birth of James Francis Edward Stuart, 'The Old Pretender': a contemporary Dutch print. Rumour had it that he was not the Queen's child but a baby smuggled in in a warming-pan. Thus originated the practice of the Home Secretary attending all royal births. The decree was waived for the births of Queen Elizabeth II's children.

His arrival coincided with the trial of the seven bishops. On 18 May Archbishop Sancroft and six of his brethren had protested against the King's order to read the Declaration of Indulgence in every church. James had treated their protest as tantamount to rebellion and had had them prosecuted for seditious libel. On 30 June they were acquitted, and the popular rejoicing far eclipsed that officially ordered for the birth of the Prince of Wales. That evening the 'invitation' which William had requested was drafted and signed. Its importance was threefold. First, it allowed William to claim that his intervention had been 'most earnestly solicited by a great many lords, both spiritual and temporal, and by many gentlemen and other subjects of all ranks'. Secondly, the seven signatories committed themselves to action on William's behalf. Danby, Devonshire and Lumley were to play leading roles in the northern risings

The Trial of the Seven Bishops

James II's efforts to convert his subjects to Catholicism met with strong resistance from many Anglican clerics, headed by the bishops of St Asaph, Bath and Wells, Bristol, Chichester, Ely and Peterborough and by the Archbishop of Canterbury. Their acquittal was greeted as a triumph of popular opinion and emphasised the weakness of James's position.

RIGHT William Sancroft, Archbishop of Canterbury: portrait by Edward Luttrel.

BELOW The bishops are conveyed to the Tower by barge along the Thames, prior to their trial: Dutch print of 1690.

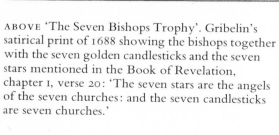

ABOVE 'The Seven Bishops Trophy'. Gribelin's
satirical print of 1688 showing the bishops together
with the seven golden candlesticks and the seven
stars mentioned in the Book of Revelation,
chapter 1, verse 20: 'The seven stars are the angels
of the seven churches: and the seven candlesticks
are seven churches.'

89

of the latter part of November, while the old soldier Bishop Compton once again buckled on his sword and escorted Princess Anne to join the rebels at Nottingham. Thirdly, they assured William that the invasion was feasible. The great majority of the people, they said, wanted a change and would join William if he landed. Not one in twenty believed that the Prince of Wales was really the King's son. Above all, they declared that the army and navy were riddled with disaffection and would refuse to fight.

The birth of James's son and the assurances in the 'invitation' emphasised both the necessity and the feasibility of invasion. There was still a strong chance, however, that events on the Continent would frustrate all William's plans. The crucial question was the behaviour of Louis XIV. To Louis, unlike William, England was of only peripheral importance. As William saw it, it was vital for both the English and the Dutch to prevent the French from overrunning the Spanish Netherlands. By the peace of Nymegen of 1678, however, Louis had got what he wanted in the Spanish Netherlands – a defensible frontier; further expansion could wait until Carlos II died. Louis had therefore switched his attention to his eastern frontier; in the following years, especially in 1683–4, he had strengthened his position in the Rhineland by means of localised and extremely brutal acts of aggression. As the attacks had been piecemeal they had not (despite William's efforts) provoked an anti-French coalition, while their extreme violence had crushed or discouraged opposition. The Emperor, on the defensive against the Turks, gave these gains temporary recognition in the Truce of Ratisbon of 1684.

Since 1684, however, the position had changed greatly. Leopold had driven the Turks back through Hungary, and late in August 1688 he took Belgrade. He was thus far more powerful than he had been in 1684; the whole European balance of power had shifted in his favour. Also, the German princes were now more determined to resist Louis's aggression and some, who had once been his clients, had now turned against him. The Dutch, too, who had been unwilling to fight in 1683–4 were now far more hostile to France. They had been shocked and disgusted by Louis's brutal persecution of the Huguenots, and their trade had been badly hit by Colbert's 'tariff war' and will take care to bring some good Ingeneers with you, and we have desired Mr. H. to consult you about all such matters, to whom we have communicated our thoughts, in many perticulars to tedious to have been written, and about which no certain resolutions can be taken, till wee have heard again from your Highnesse.

25. 24. 27. 29. 31. 35. 33.

Sh. Dev: Dany Shrews Lumley Russ. Sidney

The letter of 'invitation' sent to William: the final page, where the signatories identified themselves by number. They were: the Earl of Devonshire, Edward Russell, the Earl of Shrewsbury, the Earl of Danby, Lord Lumley, Henry Sidney and Dr Henry Compton.

against the republic. These changes had two important consequences: first, Louis felt more strongly than ever the need to consolidate his position in the Rhineland and so strengthen his German frontier; secondly, when he did so, he was likely to encounter much stiffer opposition than in 1683–4.

The likelihood that Louis would make war in 1688 and that he would do so in the Rhineland was increased by events during the year. For a long time Louis had been preparing to have a client of his elected to the key archbishopric of Cologne. In June the existing archbishop died; the election was deadlocked and referred to Rome, where the decision was expected to be in favour of the Emperor's candidate. Meanwhile, it seemed increasingly probable that Leopold would take Belgrade. If he did, there was a strong chance that the Turks would make peace, which would leave Leopold free to intervene in the west.

Louis therefore decided on several sudden, fierce 'preventive' actions – against the Rhineland fortress of Philippsburg, against Cologne and against the papal territory of Avignon. His aims were to strengthen his defensive position, to secure his candidate's election at Cologne and, if possible, to induce the Turks to fight on. To get what he wanted quickly and cheaply he relied, as in 1683–4, on speed, diplomatic threats and bluster, and the deterrent effect of extreme, concentrated brutality. He was not prepared for a protracted war, but that was what he got.

England played a very limited part in Louis's plans. After Charles II had made a separate peace with the Dutch in 1674, Louis had ceased to regard him as a useful ally and had concentrated on buying his neutrality. James II was so preoccupied with domestic affairs that he was oblivious to what happened abroad. Louis tried several times to persuade him to enter into an alliance, but James refused; he wanted no outside ties and anyway France was so unpopular that a French alliance would have seriously harmed his chances of securing an amenable Parliament. In 1688 Louis realised far sooner than James that William intended to invade England and sent full and accurate details of William's preparations; but James refused to believe him and rejected his offers of naval help. Louis then made two serious miscalculations. First he assumed that although James could be of little positive use to him, he was still strong enough to defeat William or to tie him up in a lengthy war in England. Secondly he used his usual tactic of diplomatic bluff in an effort to frighten the States General into withholding support for William's invasion. On 30 August d'Avaux presented the States with a memorial in which Louis declared that the 'bonds of friendship and alliance between him and the King of Great Britain' would oblige him to assist James in the event of an attempted invasion. The effect of the memorial was precisely the opposite of what was intended. It seemed to confirm the fears which had grown over the last couple of years (and which had been exploited by William) that the Kings of France and England were planning a joint attack on the United Provinces on the lines of that of 1672. It therefore made the States General much more willing to support William; it also greatly embarrassed James; his ambassador issued a heated denial that such an alliance existed; but nobody believed him.

ABOVE A tin-glazed plate
with a portrait of William
and Mary.

RIGHT An English dummy
board, c. 1690, showing
the life-size figure
of a man.

Five days after d'Avaux delivered his memorial, Louis attacked Philippsburg. William could now be almost certain that there would be no attack on the Dutch republic that year, and so he could complete his preparations for the invasion of England. He began his propaganda campaign, to justify his coming actions before European opinion. He did not, of course, mention that his invasion would probably end in James's deposition and William's seizing the crown. He told Leopold that he would neither dethrone James nor harm the English Catholics. Fagel told the States General that 'His highness does not intend to dethrone the king or to conquer England, but

94

Marot's impression of the departure of William's fleet from Helleveotsluys in November 1688. The fleet, in three squadrons, consisted of 225 vessels, carrying 7000 sailors.

only to ensure that by the convocation of a free parliament ... the reformed religion will be secure and out of danger.' On 30 September William issued his declaration to the English people. It consisted mainly of a long catalogue of grievances which, conventionally, were blamed on the King's evil advisers, not on the King himself. It referred to the 'pretended' Prince of Wales and stated 'that this our expedition is intended for no other design than to have a free and lawful Parliament assembled as soon as possible'.

This declaration was, of course, pure propaganda. William had no interest in English laws and liberties as such, and his experiences in the United Provinces had given him every reason to dislike representative institutions; his dislike was to be intensified by his experience of the English Parliament. He invaded because he feared that if he did not, he would lose all chance of bringing England's wealth and manpower into the great struggle against France which dominated his life. He realised from the start that he might well have to dethrone or expel James (and the Prince of Wales). Mary realised it too and prayed hard and long to nerve herself for this dreadful act of disloyalty to her father. Only the great prize of the crown could have justified the great, if calculated, risks which William took. It was very risky to undertake a major naval expedition at the beginning of winter, especially when its path was blocked by a large and well-organised fleet. It was very risky to bring over an army that was less than half the size of James's; it meant that he had to rely on the assurances of his English contacts that James's soldiers and sailors would not fight. As it happened, their judgment was not put to the test. William's fleet managed to avoid the English fleet, and James's loss of nerve meant that his soldiers' loyalty was not tried in battle. Finally, it had been risky to make detailed and expensive plans for an invasion when the whole project would have been ruined if Louis had decided to strike northwards into the republic rather than eastwards (which was what d'Avaux, for one, had urged him to do). But William's luck held and, equally important, he exploited each bit of good fortune to the full.

Only in the last week of September did James realise the danger which faced him. He hurriedly reversed his Catholicising programme and abandoned his campaign to pack Parliament.

95

ABOVE A tapestry table-
cover of the period.

LEFT Detail of the lid of an
inlaid writing cabinet.
English, late seventeenth
century.

These concessions were so obviously a response to the threat of invasion that few were convinced of their sincerity. The Tories were still disgruntled at their earlier treatment: 'Some would think one kick of the breech enough for a gentleman,' muttered one. The army was rapidly enlarged, the fleet was prepared but the militia, on which much depended, was paralysed by the disaffection of the gentlemen who were supposed to command it. Meanwhile, on 16 October William took his leave of the States General, to whom he committed the care of his wife; many tears were shed on both sides. He then bade farewell to Mary and told her that if anything happened to him she was to marry again. On the 20th he sailed, with over two hundred transport ships and an escort of about fifty warships. Next day the fleet was driven back by a storm. There were fears at first that the enterprise might have to be abandoned, but it transpired that the damage was relatively slight. It was soon repaired and then it was just a matter of waiting, waiting for the wind to veer to the east. Day after day, in England and Holland, William's friends watched the weather-cocks. Then, on 1 November, the 'Protestant wind' began to blow. William's unwieldy armada edged out into the North Sea. Its objective and William's promise were proclaimed in its banners: 'For Religion and Liberty' and '*Je Maintiendrai*'.

Wilhelm III von Oranien u.
Maria Stuart König u. Kö=
nigin von groß Brittannien
Franckreich und Irland.

4
'The Glorious Revolution' 1688-9

T<small>HE</small> 'P<small>ROTESTANT WIND</small>' played a crucial part in the Revolution. It dictated William's landing place. He had hoped originally to land in the north, where his supporters were ready to rise; but the east wind carried him through the Strait of Dover and down the Channel. He kept well clear of Portsmouth, with its large Catholic garrison, and headed further west. The wind also hampered the English fleet, which was stationed off the Essex coast, expecting William to head for the north. It was very difficult for it to sail to the east and, by the time it had got far enough to take advantage of the wind, the Dutch armada was a long way ahead. Fortune continued to favour William. On the night of 4 November the wind shifted to the west. This helped him to cut back into Torbay, which he had overshot, and drove James's fleet back to the shelter of the Kent coast. William was therefore able to land his troops and equipment unmolested.

He landed near Brixham, which to this day keeps as its own William's motto of '*Je Maintiendrai*'. The date, 5 November, conjured up memories of an earlier deliverance from Popish perils. The army soon marched off to Exeter, which it entered on the 9th, with full pomp and ceremony. The bishop and most of the city dignitaries had fled, however, and the cathedral clergy clearly disliked having Burnet in their pulpit. The common people were more welcoming, especially as William promised that all provisions would be paid for; he later had two soldiers hanged for stealing a chicken. He now waited for the nobility and gentry to come to him, as promised in the 'invitation'; but no one wanted to be first, and William became impatient. He was there at their invitation, he said; he had been obliged by his duty to God and his love for mankind to come to protect their religion, liberty and property. Where were they? A few minor figures trickled in. Then, on the 17th, there arrived Edward Seymour, perhaps the richest and most influential man in the west; two days later his great local rival, the Earl of Bath, assured William of his support. After that William's following grew rapidly: if nobody had wanted to be first, nobody wanted to be last either.

By the time James left London to join his army near Salisbury, he was already a broken man. He had reversed all his policies and had abandoned all that he had striven for. He had given the

S.K.H. Land tot Exmout-bay. His R.H. Landing at Exmouth bay.

Tories all they wanted except a free Parliament; and, as he pointed out, he could not hold free elections while a foreign army was in England. However, his Protestant subjects were by now so suspicious of their Popish king that they greatly under-estimated the value of these concessions. Moreover, the situation would change dramatically if James were to defeat William in battle. James, however, had lost the will to fight. Even before he reached his army on 19 November his nephew, Lord Cornbury, had deserted to the enemy, and news had arrived of Lord Delamere's rising in Cheshire. Soon after, Danby and his cronies seized York, and Devonshire occupied Nottingham. For several days James dithered at Salisbury, tormented by

A contemporary Dutch print showing William landing at Torbay, greeted by Englishmen. The local people put up no resistance, but rather were impressed by the spectacle.

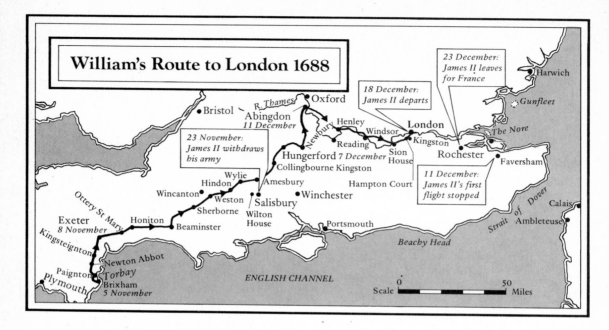

William's Route to London 1688

23 December:
James II leaves
for France

Harwich

18 December:
James II departs

Gunfleet

R. Thames Oxford

Bristol
Abingdon
11 December

Henley
Windsor   London
Reading   Kingston
Newbury   The Nore

23 November:
James II withdraws
his army

Hungerford 7 December   Sion
Collingbourne Kingston   House
                              Rochester
                                          Faversham

Wylie
Hindon   Amesbury   Hampton Court
Wincanton   Weston   11 December:
           Sherborne Salisbury Winchester   James II's first
Ottery St Mary Wilton   flight stopped
Exeter   Honiton House
8 November   Beaminster   Portsmouth   Calais
Kingsteignton   Strait of Dover Ambleteuse
                                          Beachy Head
Newton Abbot
Paignton Torbay
Plymouth Brixham   ENGLISH CHANNEL   0   50
          5 November   Scale   Miles

nosebleeds and unable to sleep. On the 21st William began to
march eastwards from Exeter, but his army was still over sixty
miles away when, on the 23rd, James decided to withdraw
without giving battle. Three of his leading colonels (Churchill,
Kirk and Grafton) then defected to William. James's army was
still much larger than William's but his nerve had gone and he
believed that he could trust nobody. On the 28th he accepted
the recommendation of an assembly of Tory notables that he
should negotiate.

William's advance became a regal progress. He took time off
to admire the Earl of Pembroke's collection of van Dycks and
on 7 December he received James's commissioners at Hungerford. The following day he stated his terms. They included the
dismissal of all Catholic officers, and the revocation of all proclamations against William and his adherents; James was to pay
William's army; James, William and their armies were to
remain at an equal distance from London and both James and
William were to attend the next session of Parliament. The
terms were hard but not unreasonable. They show that
William was prepared to leave James on the throne, though no
doubt with greatly reduced powers. This suggests that William
believed that he could persuade a free Parliament to make war

on France: he had no first-hand experience of how insular and factious English Parliaments could be. He could also be confident that a free Parliament would deal to his satisfaction with the delicate question of the legitimacy of the Prince of Wales. James, however, had no intention of accepting William's terms. He had already packed his wife and son off to France and followed them early on 11 December. William was delighted to see him go, especially as he had applied no obvious pressure: 'He was very cheerful and could not conceal his satisfaction at the King's being gone.' James's departure was followed by violent anti-Catholic riots in London, and the authorities there thought it wise to invite William to the city.

Before William could take advantage of their invitation, James was back in London. He had been stopped by some Kentish fishermen and was back at Whitehall before William could order him to stay where he was. William called a council of twelve to consider what to do with him; in such a delicate matter he preferred that the initiative should seem to come from Englishmen. In the end it was agreed that he should be allowed to escape. Dutch troops were sent to Whitehall; James was told to go to Richmond, but he asked permission to go to Rochester instead, which was readily granted. He left London on the 18th and finally sailed off to France on the 23rd. His return to London had been a great embarrassment to William. He had to use more open pressure to get rid of him the second time; James's sufferings at the hands of the fishermen aroused sympathy, and the Tories soon became convinced that William had driven him out.

With James gone, William's position was extremely strong. He had, in effect, conquered England by force of arms, but he had been careful to conceal the fact of conquest by delaying each move towards the crown until he received some sort of authorisation or invitation from a body of men in England. He carefully maintained the fiction that he was a sovereign prince who had come to save the English nation from a tyrant; he always denied that his invasion had been a rebellion. He had been lucky in that he had contracted few political debts. His supporters in James's army and navy had had no chance to show their usefulness as they had not been called upon to fight. The leaders of the northern risings had taken risks in his cause but they had not contributed materially to James's defeat and only Danby was a major political figure. Meanwhile, anti-Catholic violence up and down the country and the disorganisation caused by James's flight made it imperative to reimpose order at once, and only William had the authority to do so. An assembly of peers asked him to carry on the civil government until a convention could meet. During the elections, held early in January, William withdrew all troops from the Parliamentary boroughs. The convention thus freely elected met on 22 January 1689.

Between James's second flight and the meeting of the convention, William's popularity declined considerably. His invasion had had the active or passive support of most of the nation, but many who had supported it had not wanted to drive James out or to make William king. The Whigs were quite content; they saw William as their man and expected him to show his gratitude for their support by giving them a monopoly of power and helping them to wreak vengeance on the Tories. The Tories, however, were most uneasy. Many had accepted at face value William's promise of a free Parliament, which they had seen as the remedy for all ills. Their leaders had tried to mediate between James and William on that basis. James's flight, therefore, left them disoriented and frustrated; they greatly resented what they saw as William's undue pressure on James after his return to London. The belief soon grew that William had plotted from the outset to seize the crown and had deliberately driven James out. The Tories felt that they had been duped by false promises. Their consciences began to trouble them for having betrayed their deeply-held principles of non-resistance and passive obedience. Their rapid disillusionment with William was symbolised by a sermon to the Commons on 30 January, the anniversary of Charles I's execution; Dr John Sharp, suspended under James II for his anti-Catholic preaching, pointedly condemned the deposing of kings as a Popish practice.

The convention's main task was to settle the crown. There were five main alternatives. The first, to recall James, was supported by only a small Jacobite minority. James had, after all, deserted his followers twice. Most Tories did not want him back except on stringent conditions, to which he would be most unlikely to agree. The second possibility was that William

James, broken in spirit, flees from Whitehall: a Dutch contemporary etching. Mary felt a sense of guilt to the end of her life for her father's fate.

The Prince of ORANGE
VVelcome to LONDON.

To the Tune of, *The two English Travellers.*

P. of
Orange.

The Prince Van Orange he is come to this Land,
Who does in defiance of Popery stand:
He does not desire Supream for to Reign,
But our Laws and Liberties here to maintain.

Which some evil Persons did strive to Invade,
And we into Bondage might have been betray'd;
We see all their dealings, which troubl'd us sore,
The Fryars and Jesuits dayly came o're.

In City and Town they did Mass-houses build,
Which was with poor ignorant Proselites fill'd;
The Proverb of old is made true in this case,
We see that an ill Weed will flourish apace.

They still are inventing and forging of Lyes,
Against our Bible and Clergy likewise;
In hopes they might suddenly be overthrown;
And then they concluded the Game was their own.

The Bishops away to the Tower was sent
As stout and as chearful as Martyrs they went;
Not fearing what ever might fall to their doom,
They scorn to submit to the Clergy of Rome.

Now while the true Church thus did tottering stand,
It was a great grief to most Men in this Land:
But while we with sorrowful sighings did grieve,
Each Fryar and Jesuits laught in their Sleeve.

A broadsheet of verse, dated 1688, celebrating the arrival of the Prince of Orange and the gratitude of the English to him for maintaining their rights and liberties, and relating the events leading up to his invasion of England.

should be made sole ruler. He himself favoured this idea and it was canvassed by Bentinck, but the English would have none of it. The commander of the invasion fleet, Arthur Herbert, declared: 'I would never have drawn my sword in the Prince's favour if I could have suspected him of acting in such a way towards his wife.' Besides, by law, Mary, not William, was James's heir (leaving aside the Prince of Wales) and almost everyone wished to preserve at least the semblance of continuity and legality. Most of the High Tories supported a third expedient. Desperately anxious to avoid deposing James, they argued that his desertion and general behaviour had shown him to be incapable of ruling; the next heir, Mary, should rule as regent on his behalf. Parallels were drawn with regencies on behalf of lunatic kings in Sweden and Portugal. However, many disliked both the argument that James was insane and the separation of the powers of the Crown from the person of the King. The proposal was narrowly defeated in the Lords, so the Tories concentrated on the fourth suggestion, that Mary should be declared sole ruler. It was argued that James had 'abdicated' and that the crown had already passed by right to Mary as next heir. This removed any need for Parliament to name a successor and so prevented the introduction of an elective element into the monarchy. However, neither William nor Mary would agree to this, so the convention finally accepted the fifth alternative: that James had abdicated, that the throne was therefore vacant and that the crown should be offered jointly to William and Mary. The legal basis for such a solution was decidedly shaky, but it did fit the facts while doing as little violence as possible to deeply-held legal and constitutional beliefs and prejudices.

The controversy about the settling of the crown soon became a struggle between the predominantly Whig House of Commons and the predominantly Tory House of Lords. On 28 January the Commons voted that James had broken the original contract between king and people; by subverting the fundamental laws and withdrawing from the realm he had, in effect, abdicated, and the throne was therefore vacant. Next day the Lords rejected by two votes the proposal for a regency; they agreed that James had broken the original contract, but they decided that he had 'deserted' rather than 'abdicated'. On the 31st they voted against declaring the throne vacant and making William and Mary King and Queen. For several days the two houses were deadlocked. The Tory majority in the Lords claimed that the crown had already passed automatically to Mary and that it was not Parliament's to grant. Then Mary wrote to Danby that she would not become Queen unless William was made King. William then summoned three leading members of the Lords. 'He had not', he told them, 'come over to establish a commonwealth [republic] or to be a duke of

Venice.' He refused to 'have any share in the government unless it was put in his person and that for the term of his life'. He 'would not be his wife's gentleman usher'. He added that he would accept Anne as his heir if Mary had no children. The Lords had little choice but to give in; as Halifax remarked, 'He might do as he pleased, for as nobody knew what to do with him, so no one knew what to do without him.' He already exercised executive power and was in a position to dictate terms; but he preferred, as always, the fiction of an unsolicited invitation. Parliament for its part preserved at least an outward show of legality by insisting that Mary should be made joint ruler; but no one doubted that the real power would lie with William. On 6 February, then, the Lords bowed to the inevitable and agreed that James had abdicated. A week later William and Mary were formally offered the crown.

In the debates on the offer of the crown, Tories and Whigs shared the same basic assumptions. Both believed in the perfection of the traditional system of law and government, the 'ancient constitution'. Both believed that James II had flagrantly and repeatedly violated it in a dastardly attempt to impose Popery and absolutism. But the ancient constitution assumed that the king would operate within the law; it provided no remedy for the subject if the king bent or broke the law and refused to heed the petitions of his Parliament. The Whigs, drawing on the arguments of Parliament during the civil war, argued that in the last resort the law of self-preservation operated and that the subject had the right to resist a tyrant. The Tories argued that it was wrong to meet royal illegality with the even greater illegality of rebellion; they claimed that the horrors of the Interregnum had shown that the consequences of resistance were even worse than those of excessive royal power. Whigs and Tories therefore gave different answers to the question which faced them in 1689: did the fact that James II had violated the constitution, and was likely to do so again given half the chance, justify Parliament's violating the same constitution by deposing him and putting someone else in his place? The Whigs argued that the replacement of one monarch by another was not only justifiable in this case but had already happened; it only remained for Parliament to recognise the fact. It was more important to preserve the spirit of the constitu-

tion than to observe its precise forms; they were altering the constitution far less than James would have done.

The Tories' attitude was both more emotional and more legalistic. They revered the monarchy both as an integral part of the ancient constitution and as a sacred institution, ordained by God and hallowed by the Church. They therefore believed that for subjects to put one king in another's place was both illegal and a sin in the sight of God. However laudable these scruples might be, they broke down in practice. The great weakness of Tory political theory was that it provided no remedy but passive submission if the king broke the law or attacked the Church. But events in 1688, especially the seven bishops' petition, had shown only too clearly that in the last resort the Tories were not prepared to remain passive. However

A sheet of lining paper taken from a travelling trunk of 1688. The English woodcut design illustrates 'The Five Senses'.

much they might dislike it, their resistance had helped to expel James and bring in William. Their legitimism, therefore, although theoretically consistent, was unrealistic: few Tories wanted James back except on conditions that he would not accept; even William was better than James with a French army at his back.

The debates of 1689 are usually depicted as a conflict between progressive and enlightened Whigs and reactionary Tories, between the proponents of 'contractual' monarchy and of 'divine right' monarchy. As already suggested, however, the constitutional outlooks of Whigs and Tories had much in common. There were Tories who believed in an original contract: some form of contract was implicit in the assumption that the king should govern according to law and in his coronation oath. On the other hand, hardly anyone believed in 'divine right', in the sense of a belief that kings were above the law. James I qualified his pontifications on the divine attributes of kingship with an insistence that kings should always govern within the law; he, Charles I, even James II always observed the forms of law, as interpreted by their judges. The Tories, then, believed in 'divine right' in the vaguer and more limited sense of respecting the sanctity of both the monarch's person and the hereditary succession. The trouble with the Tories' political ideas was not that they were bad or wrong but that they simply fell apart in the face of the extraordinary behaviour of James II.

Meanwhile, two factors made the Whigs' political ideas seem more modern and rational than they really were. First, they fitted the facts of the situation in 1689. Secondly, the principles which underlay the Revolution were soon to be embodied in a coherent political theory by John Locke. Locke's *Two Treatises of Government* had been written almost a decade before the Revolution but it was not published until 1690. However, Locke's cool, rational deductions from first principles were not at all typical of Whig political writing before or even after 1689. In particular Locke abandoned what had previously been the mainstay of Whig and Parliamentarian arguments, the appeal to history and to the ancient constitution, which was said to date back to time immemorial, unchanged, unchanging and unchangeable. In the works of men like William Prynne or William Petyt, the enunciation of general principles was far less

Clocks of the reign of
William and Mary:
OPPOSITE A long-case
clock decorated with
marquetry and a walnut
veneer.
LEFT A bracket clock by
John Knibb. It is made of
oak with an ebony veneer.

apparent than the regurgitation of great chunks of bogus
history and bad law, often backed up by vicious anti-Catholic-
ism. From this tangle of the rational and the irrational and, more
important, from the experience of the civil war, had grown the
concepts of the right of resistance and of the original contract
which enabled the Whigs to accept William's accession without
demur. Within the context of debates in 1689, in terms of the
ancient constitution, the Tories had a better case than most later

historians have recognised. But events had gone against them; they had little choice but to swallow their scruples; at least they could look forward to Anne as William's successor.

Although he tried to maintain a show of indifference, William was very irritated by what he regarded as the Lords' pedantic reluctance to bow to the inevitable. 'If I were not so scrupulous by nature, I should not hesitate to wind up the affair at once;' he wrote, 'the only consolation I have is that, God knows, it is

The Declaration of Rights being read to William and Mary prior to their coronation: an engraving from an eighteenth-century history of England. It affirmed the rights of the citizen and of Parliaments, which the Stuarts had lately violated.

not ambition that rules me.' At last, however, all was settled and Mary was summoned to England. Her feelings in these last weeks had been very mixed. She had been elated at William's success but felt sorry for James: 'I cannot forget my father and I grieve for his misfortune.' She was saddened by the thought of 'leaving a country where I had the esteem of the inhabitants, where I had led a life so suitable to my humour and, as I think, not unacceptable to my God, where, in a word, I had all earthly content'. She sought consolation in prayer and worship and watched vigilantly for the signs of pride or vanity which would show that the devil was at work in her heart. On 11 February she arrived in England. She was reunited with William amid floods of tears. She was worried to find him very pale and coughing blood, but he told her to appear cheerful. She rather overdid it, and was criticised for her apparent levity and lack of feeling towards her father. On 13 February William and Mary received the Lords and Commons in the Banqueting House at Whitehall. The Declaration of Rights was read to them and they were asked to accept the crown. William replied: 'We thankfully accept what you have offered us' and promised to rule according to law and to be guided by Parliament. He and Mary were then proclaimed King and Queen.

The Declaration of Rights was the keystone of the constitutional settlement and has an important place in British and American history; but it was in some ways an odd document. It was not made clear whether the offer of the crown depended on William's accepting the Declaration or whether it was simply read for his information. This ambiguity was largely removed when Parliament passed it as the Bill of Rights in December 1689 and William gave it the royal assent. The Declaration had little coherent political theory behind it; it was a pragmatic document, dealing in a practical way with a variety of practical problems. It had two main purposes: first, to ratify the change of monarch and to draw certain practical conclusions from it and, secondly, to condemn certain abuses of royal power by Charles II and James II.

First the succession. The Declaration told of James's 'abdication' and the declaration that William and Mary were King and Queen. It fixed the succession after their deaths: first Mary's children, if any, then Anne and her heirs and finally any children

William might have by a later marriage. It declared that no Catholic, or wife or husband of a Catholic, could become King or Queen of England. It also imposed a new oath of allegiance, to be taken by office-holders, MPs and clergymen. In deference to Tory scruples, it avoided referring to William and Mary as 'rightful and lawful' monarchs. Most Tory laymen took it but an important minority of the clergy (the 'non-jurors') refused, including six bishops.

Secondly, the constitutional provisions. While clarifying certain disputed points, the Declaration imposed only one novel restriction on the prerogative: the assertion that 'The raising or keeping a standing army within the kingdom in time of peace, unless it be with the consent of Parliament, is against law.' The army's legal status had hitherto been uncertain, although it had been accepted that the king had sole direction of the army, navy and militia; now his control of the army in peacetime was considerably restricted. It was not this one new restriction, however, which made the Declaration important to later generations, but the safeguards which it tried to provide for the rights and liberties of both Parliaments and subjects. It asserted that subjects had a right to petition the king, that Parliamentary debates and elections should be free and that Parliament should meet regularly. Some of its most important provisions reflect the experience of Charles II and James II's extensions of the prerogative and their use of the law courts as instruments of political manipulation and vengeance. It condemned the suspending and dispensing powers, the packing of juries, the exaction of excessive fines or bail and 'cruel and unusual punishments'. One major consequence of the Revolution was the separation of the law from politics and the freeing of judges from political pressures; William showed great restraint and good sense in refraining from interference in the processes of justice. By doing so, he ensured that the ideals of the Declaration should become a reality, and made possible the Revolution's great achievement: the vindication of the rule of law and the protection of the law-abiding individual against the state. It was this which led to the incorporation of some of the Declaration's provisions into the United States constitution, where they still have an impact on American life. The right to bear arms, guaranteed to Americans by the Second Amendment, was guaranteed to English Protestants by the Bill of Rights. The prohibition of 'cruel and unusual punishments' by the Eighth Amendment has recently been cited in an argument before the Supreme Court that the death penalty is unconstitutional – although in 1689 no one would have regarded it as either cruel or unusual to hang people for trivial offences against property. If the phrase has changed its meaning over the centuries, it has not lost its relevance; nor indeed have many of the other provisions of the Declaration.

The Crown's prerogatives were gradually whittled away after 1689, but not by the Bill of Rights. The Triennial Act of 1694 curtailed the king's power to summon and dismiss Parliaments at will by laying down that there should be a general election at least once every three years. The Act of Settlement of 1701, besides securing the Hanoverian succession, imposed some irritating restrictions on the future German King, which reflected the Tories' hatred of William rather than memories of James II. The most important check on the Crown was not imposed by legislation at all. In 1689 Parliament, contrary to precedent, refused to grant the incoming King a revenue for life that was sufficient to enable him to 'live of his own'. In Burnet's words, 'It was taken up as a general maxim that a revenue for a certain and short term was the best security that the nation could have for frequent Parliaments.' William was furious. He told Burnet that 'He was not a king till that was done; without that the title of a king was only a pageant ... the worst of all governments was that of a king without a treasure and without power.' He told Halifax that 'The Commons used him like a dog.' Always concerned with the realities of power rather than its outward forms, William saw clearly that shortage of money would restrict his direction of the war effort far more than the provisions of the Bill of Rights could do. But there was nothing he could do; Parliament held the whip hand.

It was the King's dependence on Parliament for money which really altered the position of the monarchy and the working of politics after 1689. This dependence was completed by the war. Vast sums had to be raised by taxation and borrowing. Parliament came increasingly to supervise the spending as well as the raising of money. By the end of the war, Parliament

' The Commons used him like a dog'

The coronation of
William and Mary in
Westminster Abbey on
11 April 1689: an
engraving by de Hooghe
illustrating the various
stages of the ceremony.
Russell reported that 'this
was much finer and in
better order' than James's
coronation, 'and if the
number of ladies were
fewer, yet their attendance
was with more application
near the Queen all the
time, and with more
cheerful faces by
a great deal.'

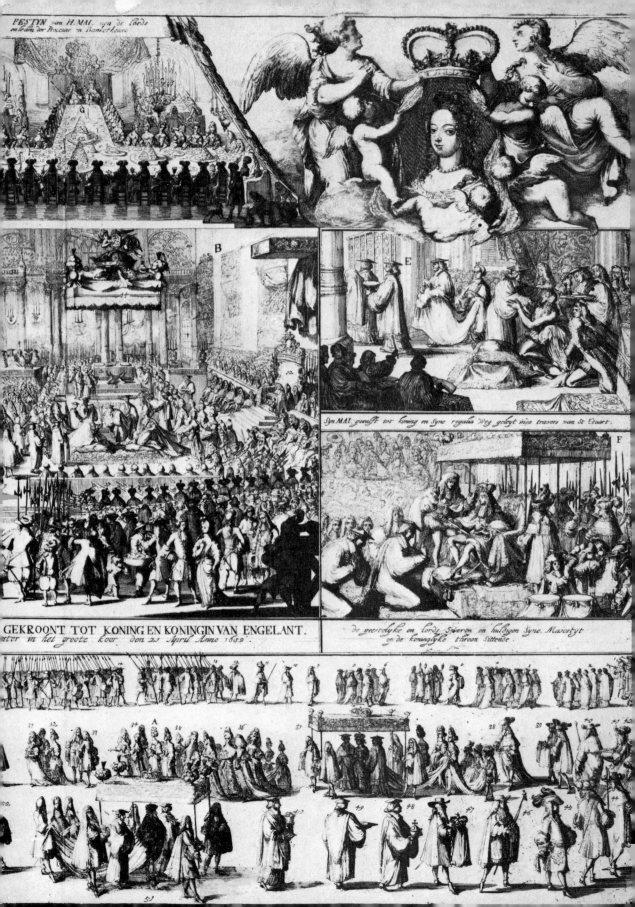

FESTYN van H. MAI. aen de Lords en leden der Processie in Bankethouse

GEKROONT TOT KONING EN KONINGIN VAN ENGELANT.
...ster in het groote koor den 21 April Anno 1689.

Syn MAI. gesalft tot koning en Syne regalia Weg geleyt inde travers van St Eduart.

de geestelyke en lords Sweren en hulbigen Syne Majestyt op de koninglyke throon Sittende

Medal with portraits of
William and Mary
designed by George
Bower. Below is a
facsimile of their
signatures.

had gained overall control of military and naval expenditure;
the King's financial independence was now limited to the civil
administration, for which he was voted a lump sum, the 'civil
list'. The threat, implicit or explicit, that Parliament might
refuse or delay supplies of money forced the King to pay far
more attention to its criticisms of his administration. Parliament also met more frequently, and the management of
Parliament became the main concern of the King's ministers.
Apart from arranging the agenda and putting forward government policies, they also had to provide rewards for government
supporters – jobs for MPs and their relatives, titles, pensions and
bribes. The number of such rewards available increased greatly
after 1689: as the volume of taxation increased, so the nation's

financial administration grew, and the armed forces were also much larger than before. The main threat to Parliament's independence after the Revolution came not from the Crown's *prerogative*, which was now effectively circumscribed, but from its actual or potential *influence* – its ability to win over MPs by means of rewards and favours. These changes owed little or nothing to the pious platitudes of the Bill of Rights; they had their roots in the refusal to grant William a permanent revenue and in the financial changes caused by the wars.

One final achievement of the Revolution was the Toleration Act of 1689, the first statutory grant of religious toleration in England. This was virtually forced on the convention by the much fuller liberty granted by James II. It repealed none of the existing penal laws, but laid down that certain Dissenters should not suffer the penalties of certain laws. These had to be Protestants who were willing to take the new oath of allegiance and affirm their belief in the Trinity. Those who did were to be allowed to meet publicly under certain conditions; but if they wished to hold public office, they had to qualify by taking the sacrament according to the rites of the Church of England. The act gave Protestant Dissenters religious liberty but not political equality. In practice, the religious liberty was extended to Catholics as well; William refused to order the enforcement of the penal laws against them. He kept that part of his promise to Leopold.

The Toleration Act ended the Church of England's monopoly of the nation's religious life, a monopoly which had been no more than theoretical since the Interregnum. It did not lead to a great increase in the number of Dissenters, but it did permanently weaken the Church, especially in the towns; in the countryside the combined authority of parson and squire could still drive the people to church. Religious pluralism became a fact of English life, especially after the abolition of Press censorship in 1695. Hitherto government and Church had tried to suppress works which encouraged either political disaffection or religious heterodoxy. Now books appeared by men like John Toland, who attacked the very foundations of revealed religion. Needless to say, High Anglicans resented these developments. They disliked William anyway as a usurper: even those who took the oath of allegiance had strong emotional sympathies with the non-jurors. In 1688–9 William had also snubbed the High Churchmen and gone out of his way to show favour to the Presbyterians. There were other causes of resentment too: the appointment of the Whiggish Burnet as Bishop of Salisbury, and the establishment of Presbyterianism and persecution of episcopalian clergy in Scotland. All were blamed, fairly or unfairly, on Calvinist Dutch William. The Churchmen looked forward with unconcealed impatience to the accession of the staunchly Anglican Anne.

As 1689 wore on, William's popularity slumped still further. Many believed that if James would only abandon his Catholicism, he could easily recover his throne. William found breathing difficult in the damp and smoggy air of London and moved out to Hampton Court, far from the centre of fashionable life. He made little effort to win over the English aristocracy and was soon accused of being stand-offish. As early as the end of January John Evelyn noted that he 'showed little countenance to the noblemen and others, who expected a more gracious and cheerful reception when they made their court'. He disliked crowds anyway, found spoken English hard to follow and had little in common with English aristocrats who were far more interested in agriculture than in war. As Burnet wrote:

> He gave too much occasion to a general disgust, which was spread both among the English officers and the nobility; he took little pains to gain the affections of the nation; nor did he constrain himself enough to render his government more acceptable: he was shut up all the day long: and his silence, when he admitted any to an audience, distasted them as much as if they had been denied it.

He surrounded himself with Dutchmen like Zuylestein, Ouwerkerk and the ever-faithful Bentinck, now Earl of Portland. He admitted few Englishmen to his confidence, apart from Sidney and Halifax: 'The king was thought to love the Dutch more than the English, to trust more to them and to admit them to more freedom with him.' The Dutch, for their part, longed to go home. They found England 'a devilish country, so dirty and wicked'. William was homesick and miserable; he coughed incessantly and even started talking to himself.

Mary too was unhappy. She was criticised for her apparent indifference when she took over her father's throne and palaces:

like a good housewife, she immediately investigated all the cupboards. At first everybody paid their court to her, but when they found that she had no political influence, many stopped doing so. She found herself 'very much neglected, little respected, censured of all, commended by none'. She spent much time, as always, at her devotions and threw herself into planning the rebuilding of Hampton Court. She also persuaded William to buy Kensington House, which was rather nearer London. But she was still not happy. She described her first year as Queen as 'a year of trial in every way'. 'I still love Holland', she wrote sadly, 'and I shall always remember the tranquillity I enjoyed there and that I shall never find here.'

If the English aristocracy was disillusioned with William, he was driven to distraction by English politicians. Once the crown had been settled, they reverted, as usual, to faction fighting and scrambling for office. William was in a dilemma. The Whigs had supported his elevation to the throne, but he distrusted them as neo-republicans and was disgusted by the vindictiveness of their pursuit of the ministers of Charles II and James II. He much preferred the Tories, as the natural supporters of monarchy, but they hated him as a usurper and enemy of

A lace box made in walnut in 1692.

A ewer or decanter jug
made of clear colourless
'crizzled' glass engraved on
a wheel. It is English with
Dutch engraving, and
dates from c. 1680–5.

the Church. He compromised by appointing a mixed ministry, which satisfied nobody. The Tories claimed that the Whigs were republicans, the Whigs accused the Tories of Jacobitism. The administration was riddled with corruption and ineptitude, and Parliament was so slow to vote money that the campaigning season came and went with little being done. The danger from the Scots Jacobites ended with the battle of Dunkeld in August, but in Ireland the Protestants were in desperate straits, to which Parliament seemed largely indifferent. William was so depressed that at one point he even threatened to return to Holland, leaving Mary to rule England; his ministers persuaded him to stay. By January 1690 he had had enough of the convention; he prorogued and later dissolved it, dismissed his more extreme Whig ministers and announced his intention of going to Ireland.

5 Orange Triumph

in Ireland 1689-90

T HE SEVENTEENTH CENTURY was a vital period in the history of Ireland. The English conquest had started in the twelfth century, but it was not until the latter part of Elizabeth's reign that English rule began to extend beyond the Pale, the area immediately around Dublin. This imposition of effective authority paved the way for the establishment of Protestant ascendancy during the seventeenth century, to which William applied the finishing touches. The legacy of the Scots and English plantations and of the establishment of Protestant dominance can still be seen in Ulster today. William's importance, real and symbolic, can be illustrated by the reverence or hatred with which his memory is regarded by Irish Protestants and Catholics.

By the end of the seventeenth century the basic division in Irish society was that between Protestants and Catholics but that had not been so at the beginning. In 1600 the Protestant officials and settlers formed only a tiny minority of the population, but even by 1640 the situation had changed. Much of the land in six counties of mid and west Ulster was declared forfeit to the Crown after the flight to the Continent of the Earls of Tyrone and Tyrconnel in 1607; many English and Scots settlers moved into these counties while the native Irish remained as tenants and labourers. The two eastern counties of Down and Antrim were more intensively settled by Lowland Scots who made the short journey across the North Channel. By 1640 Ulster had changed from the most Gaelic to the most Protestant part of Ireland; the fact that so many of the settlers were Scots Presbyterians was to lead to serious conflicts within the Irish Protestant community, between the Presbyterians and the English, episcopalian Church of Ireland.

The Catholics were similarly divided. The great majority were native Irish, but many of the nobility and gentry were 'Old English', the heirs of the original Anglo-Norman conquerors. Their names were English (Butler, Talbot and the like) and they had a long tradition of loyalty to the English Crown. Between 1603 and 1641 they were made increasingly uneasy by the English government's efforts to squeeze more revenue out of Ireland and by its sporadic attempts to persecute the Catholics. Then, in 1641, the native Irish of Ulster suddenly rose in rebellion against English rule. The Old English were torn

PREVIOUS PAGES The siege of Londonderry which ended on 31 July 1689: from a contemporary Dutch engraving. It had lasted 105 days.

126

Richard Talbot, Earl of Tyrconnel: portrait attributed to H. Rigaud. When William came to the throne, Tyrconnel was Lord Deputy of Ireland, having built up a strong Catholic force there.

between their loyalty to England and their loyalty to their religion. After much hesitation they threw in their lot with the rebels, not least because they feared that their Irish tenants might rise against them if they did not. It was a fateful decision, for it was to give the victorious Parliamentarians a pretext to treat all Catholics as rebels.

Confused fighting continued for over ten years. Only under Cromwell and his successors was the last Catholic and Royalist resistance extinguished. The Cromwellian land settlement followed; under it virtually every Catholic and Royalist Protestant landowner was to forfeit all or part of his estates.

127

Those proprietors who were to retain some land were to be transported into Connaught, beyond the Shannon, where they were to receive land in proportion to their remaining property. Their lands were to go partly to disbanded English soldiers, in lieu of their arrears of pay, and partly to the 'Adventurers' – Englishmen who had advanced money to Parliament in the 1640s on the security of future confiscations of Irish land. The settlement was intended both to pay the English government's debts at the expense of the Irish rebels and to strengthen the Protestant population of Ireland, so that the Catholics could be held in check. These aims were not entirely fulfilled, but even so the impact of the settlement was enormous. In 1641 Catholics had owned about sixty per cent of the land; by 1660 they owned only eight or nine per cent. The Protestants were still a minority, although their numbers had increased greatly since the start of the century. In 1672 it was estimated that there were eight hundred thousand Catholics and three hundred thousand Protestants; only about a third of the Protestants were Church of Ireland, most of the rest being Presbyterians.

At the Restoration Charles II was torn between his desire to restore the Irish Catholics' lands and the need to retain the political support of the Protestants. The Restoration land settlement, embodied in the Acts of Settlement and Explanation, was therefore an uneasy compromise; on the whole it left the Cromwellians in possession but allowed some fortunate Catholics to recover their lands. This was a gradual process, but by 1685 the amount of land in Catholic hands had risen to a little over twenty per cent. The main division in Ireland was now that between Catholic and Protestant; there might be tensions between English and Scots, between Church of Ireland and Presbyterians, but they were soon forgotten if any danger threatened from the Catholics; memories of the 1641 rebellion were still vivid. For their part, Old English and native Irish Catholics were driven together by common misery and deprivation. They were not usually persecuted, but they were systematically excluded from public offices and political power, in Parliament and the municipalities; and, of course, they had lost their lands, apart from a minority who had influential friends or who were simply lucky. Under Charles II, then, the Catholics were bitter about the past, but they could look forward to the prospect of a Catholic king; then all might change.

When James II became King, he tried to pursue two incompatible objectives in Ireland. On one hand, he wanted to allow the Catholics religious freedom and to admit them to civil and military office; on the other hand, he did not want to alarm or antagonise his Protestant subjects in either Ireland or England. He therefore gave repeated assurances that the Act of Settlement would be retained and early in 1686 he sent over a moderate Protestant, the Earl of Clarendon, as Lord Lieutenant. Both James and Clarendon were too moderate for the Irish Catholics, however, and they found a spokesman in Richard

'Roaring Dick' Talbot, a close friend of James's since the 1650s, who was created Earl of Tyrconnel in 1685. He was less extreme than many of the Catholics – he wanted to repeal the Act of Settlement, but only with substantial compensation for the Cromwellians – but his behaviour alarmed the Protestants. He was, in Clarendon's words, 'a man of monstrous vanity as well as pride and furious passion'; his remark that 'these acts of settlement and this new interest are damned things' was hard to reconcile with the King's assurances that the Act would be preserved. As time went on, Tyrconnel's control of Irish affairs became complete and the pace of Catholicisation quickened. Protestants were turned out of the army – 'I would have all the Catholics in', said Tyrconnel – so that by the end of 1688 it was almost wholly Catholic.

'*A man of monstrous vanity as well as pride and furious passion*'

At first James tried to keep a balance between Catholics and Protestants in the civil administration, but Catholics soon came to predominate. A campaign against borough charters prepared the way for the election of a Catholic Parliament. Protestants were not excluded from office, especially where special skills were needed, as in the revenue administration. Ten of the twenty-four aldermen of Dublin were Protestants, but the Protestants were usually in the minority and they were especially alarmed when Tyrconnel became Lord Deputy in 1687. Their alarm was described in the song *Lillibulero*:

> Ho brother Teague, dost hear de decree
> Dat we shall have a new deputy.
> Ho by my soul it is a Talbot
> And he will cut all de English throat, etc.

Even in 1686 Protestant merchants began to sell up and sail for England; the exodus accelerated in 1687–8.

When William invaded England in 1688, Tyrconnel controlled Ireland. As William was fully occupied in England, he could do nothing to help the Irish Protestants who now organised to defend themselves. Instead he entered into negotiations with Tyrconnel, which came to nothing. In February 1689, therefore, William formally called on the Irish 'rebels' to lay down their arms; he offered religious liberty and security of property to those who did so and threatened to confiscate the estates of those who did not. He could do nothing more, however, and by mid-March the Catholics controlled all of Ireland, except Londonderry and Enniskillen. Meanwhile, James came over from France in a bid to recover his kingdoms. In April he summoned the people of Derry to surrender; they refused and a long and bitter siege began. James's army lacked the artillery and the mining tools it needed to force a breach, so it blockaded the city in an effort to starve it into submission. A boom was stretched across Lough Foyle to stop relief ships from reaching the city. In England the position seemed hopeless; over thirty thousand people were crowded within the walls, racked by hunger and disease. Help from England took an agonising time to arrive, and when some ships did appear, it was six weeks before they tried to break the boom. Finally, on 28 July, the boom was cut and two ships, laden with food, sailed into the city. Three days later the siege broke up. The same day the men of Enniskillen, who had harassed the besiegers most effectively, crushed a Jacobite army at Newtown Butler. Ulster was saved.

Meanwhile, the alienation of the Irish Protestants had been completed by the Parliament which James held in Dublin. It ignored his pleas for moderation and gave full vent to the Catholics' accumulated hatred of all things Protestant and English. It repealed the Act of Settlement; it voted that the English Parliament could not legislate for Ireland; and it passed an Act of Attainder, containing 2,400 names, which would have dispossessed virtually every Protestant landowner in Ireland. This was the Catholics' revenge for the Cromwellian settlement; it ensured that the Protestants in their turn would impose an equally vindictive settlement when they regained power.

It is unlikely that the Jacobite army had either the skill or the resources to take Derry. It is certain, however, that the stubborn courage of the people of Derry and the Enniskilliners' victory at Newtown Butler saved the Protestants' position in Ireland. They now controlled most of Ulster, so William's army had a firm base from which to start reconquering the country. Having failed to win a quick victory, the Jacobites had to prepare for a long war, in which their weaknesses became increasingly apparent. Once the resources of England were fully brought to bear on Ireland, the Jacobites' chances of victory were nil, although the stubbornness of their resistance was to deny the Williamites victory for some time.

Furniture in the Reign of William and Mary

Post-Restoration furniture was largely
influenced in design by French and Dutch
models, though the luxury items made for the
English Court in this period were not
generally available. In the country and the
provinces the simpler, earlier styles prevailed.

BELOW A lacquered cabinet on a silvered
stand. Late seventeenth century.

LEFT A walnut cabinet, decorated with marquetry and showing William on horseback in the top section. It dates from 1688.
BELOW A late seventeenth-century English chair featuring turned and carved walnut.

The Jacobites' problems started at the top. James never got over the shock of 1688. The qualities of decisiveness and leadership which he had shown in his youth had now deserted him. While he dithered and bumbled, his French and Irish advisers allowed their feuds and rivalries full play, so the military command was confused and unco-ordinated. As for the soldiers, they were enthusiastic enough, especially when drunk or when stirred up by their priests, but their military value was doubtful. Many units had been hastily raised and lacked discipline; 'They will follow none but their own leaders', noted one observer, 'many of them men as rude, as ignorant and as far from understanding any of the rules of discipline as themselves.' Some officers had served abroad but most were totally inexperienced. (The Irish army had been entirely Protestant under Charles II.) The army was also desperately short of equipment. Most soldiers lacked uniforms; many were dressed in rags and had no shoes. There was little artillery and few muskets; one regiment at the siege of Derry had only seven muskets. There were not even enough pikes, so many men had half-pikes, daggers or sickles. The army lived off the country, partly because nobody took responsibility for military administration but mainly because the army had hardly any supplies. It had no money either; it cost £100,000 a month, but the Dublin Parliament voted only one fifth of that amount, and much of the money was not collected. Ireland was a poor country and it was made poorer by the burning of towns and fields and by the interruption of trade and agriculture during the war. Desperately short of cash, James's government debased the currency, issuing brass coins and even melting down brass guns to make them. But the situation still grew worse; prices rose, despite efforts to hold them down, while the depredations of the army weakened the economy further. It was the much greater wealth of England as much as William's military skill which ensured his victory.

William also faced serious military problems in 1689, but they were not of the same order of magnitude and, unlike James's, they were likely to become less serious with time. The Revolution had disorganised the English army; many units went home or were disbanded and the loyalty of others was suspect: there were several mutinies in 1689. William kept his Dutch troops in England, sent the best English units to Flanders and then began to raise new regiments to send to Ireland. Secondly, the military administration combined inefficiency and corruption on a massive scale; Henry Shales, the commissary general, later proved unable to account for some £70,000 which had passed through his hands. The army sent to Ireland in 1689, therefore, included a high proportion of inexperienced officers and men (with some more experienced Huguenots and Dutch) and much of its equipment and provisions was defective or failed to materialise.

These problems made its veteran commander Schomberg even more cautious than usual; his letters to William were full of complaints. He did clear the Jacobites out of most of their remaining positions in Ulster, but when he came face to face with James's army near Dundalk he declined to fight. He was unwilling to trust many of his troops in a major battle, especially as a defeat at this stage would seriously jeopardise the Protestants' position. He therefore retreated to Lisburn where his army spent a wet and miserable winter. Many of the men lacked proper shelters, or were too inept or lazy to build them. Food and medical supplies ran short. Over seven thousand men, more than half Schomberg's army, died of disease and exposure during the winter.

Schomberg's expedition showed that the military administration needed a drastic overhaul, so William took charge of it himself. It also showed that a full-scale military operation was needed if the Irish problem was not to drag on and on. William therefore decided to go to Ireland himself; otherwise 'nothing worthwhile would be done'. His decision was greeted with dismay. Mary did not want 'to see my husband and my father personally engaged against each other'. His ministers feared that the French might try to invade England while he was away. Parliament procrastinated, taking weeks to vote the necessary money and to agree to the arrangements for a regency council, headed by Mary, to rule England in his absence. But William had made up his mind and he was determined to leave nothing to chance; he aimed, for once, to have overwhelmingly superior forces and crush the Jacobites in a single campaign. His preparations were much more thorough than those of the previous year. Including some Irish Protestant regiments, he was to have an army of almost forty-four thousand men, with a large siege

'My husband and my father personally engaged against each other'

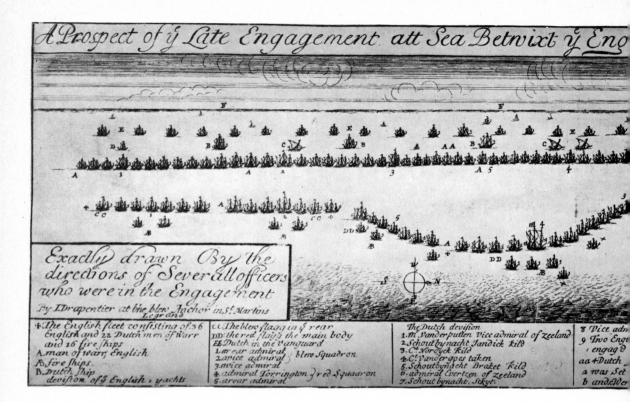

train and ample supplies (including £200,000 in cash). Unless
he made some disastrous blunder, therefore, the outcome of the
campaign could not be in doubt. William's health and spirits
grew better and better. He loved war – 'He was sure that he
understood that better than how to govern England' – and was
warmly received by the people on his way to Chester. He sailed
on 11 June, and three days later landed on the Irish coast near
Carrickfergus.

Within days William, eager for battle, began to march south.
Meanwhile, James had emerged from his lethargy and had sent
his army northwards. When it reached Dundalk, James heard
of William's arrival. He then fell back to defend the southern
bank of the River Boyne, just west of Drogheda. On 30 June
William's army reached the northern bank. It was much larger
than James's (about thirty-six thousand as against twenty-five
thousand), its artillery and equipment were superior and its
infantry (which included Huguenots, Danes, Brandenburgers
and even Finns) was far more experienced. James's army (which

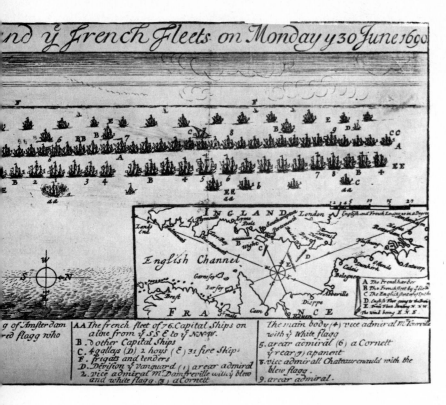

now included a French contingent) had only one real advantage,
an excellent defensive position. The river could be forded when
the tide was right, but it would not be easy in the face of enemy
fire. James therefore drew up his army at Donore, on high
ground which commanded the most obvious crossing place, at
Oldbridge. Throughout the 30th the armies faced each other
across the river; it was said that William would not fight
because he was superstitious about fighting on Mondays. There
was some sporadic artillery fire on both sides and a cannon-ball
grazed William's right shoulder. A great shout went up on the
Jacobite side when he fell and news was sent post-haste to
France that he was dead; there was great rejoicing at Paris, and
he and Mary were burned in effigy. In fact, the wound was
slight. 'It's well it came no nearer,' said William laconically, and
he rode the whole length of his army waving his sword in his
right hand to show that no great harm had been done.

James had known all along that his chances of victory were
slim; after a flicker of hope when William was wounded, his

OVERLEAF Another
broadsheet of verses to be
sung, illustrating popular
feeling towards the new
Protestant king, and
particularly after his
victory over the Irish at
the Boyne and his
triumphant entry
into Dublin.

THE
Proteſtant Triumph:

OR,

The ſignal Victory of K. *William* over the *French* and *Iri[ſh]*

Chaſing them from Hill to Hill, taking their Arms and Ammunition alſo; t[he]
Surrender of *Drogheda*, and the King's entring the City of *Dublin*; to the u[n]
ſpeakable Joy and Satisfaction of all True Proteſtants.

This Victory was obtain'd on Tueſday the Firſt of July 1690.

To the Tune of The Spinning wheel.   Licenſed according to Order.

BRave Boys, let Bells now ſweetly ring.
  and flowing Bowls go freely roun',
With Healths to our moſt gracious King,
  who is this day with Triumph Crown'd:
A Fig for all our Romiſh Foes,
K. William Conquers where he goes.

While Trumpets ſounded Victory,
  and rattling Warlike Drums did beat;
We laugh'd to ſee the Tories flee,
  in what Confuſion they retreat,
While we purſu'd with hardy Blows,
K. William Conquers where ſhe goes.

The French and Torys hearts did ake,
  as ſoon as ever we drew near,
And did their Paſſes ſoon forſake,
  being glad to run away for fear:
They knew they could not us oppoſe,
K. William Conquers where he goes.

To Ardee Paſs we march'd with ſpeed,
  where many Thouſand Tories lay,
Who being the right Iriſh Breed,
  they tuck to heels and run away:
K. William he ſuch Courage ſhows,
Which Conquers all where e'er he goes.

ur right renowned King reply'd,
  March on, my valiant warlike Boys,
oz we shall soon subdue the Pride
  of both the French and the Dear-joys:
hus did he Chase his flying Foes,
  and Conquers all where e'er he goes.

ing William Marching in the Head,
  while Trumpets did most sweetly sound,
nd all our flying Colours spread,
  which fight did all our Foes confound:
. William's Courage scares his Foes,
e Conquers all where e'er he goes.

t length we had a bloody Fray,
  our Guns like Thunder then did roar,
. William he did win the day,
  and laid the French in reeking Goze:
is Courage scares his mighty Foes,
e conquers all where e'er he goes.

Now while the Fight we did maintain,
  we made the Tozy Rebells rue ;
ozd Carlingford he being slain,
  and many Great Commanders too :
. William's Courage daunts his Foes,
e Conquers all where e'er he goes.

Stout Colonel Parker, with his Teagues,
  likewise lay bleeding on the Ground,
We scour'd them foz their late Intrieguing;
  while our King is with Trophies Crown'd:
To Dublin Gates he chas'd his Foes,
He Conquers all where e'er he goes.

The King he sent to Drogheda,
  to yield before it was too late ;
Oz else his roaring Guns he'd play,
  with that they did surrender straft ;
Now they could not him oppose,
VVho Conquers all where e'er he goes.

Late James he quitted Dublin straight
And great King William did march in,
'Tis joyfull Tydings to relate,
  how he do's Fame and Honour win:
His Courage scares the mighty Foes,
He Conquers, &c.

Poz Protestants he did free,
  which in close Prisons long hath lain,
They all enjoy their Liberty,
  under K. VVilliam who do's Reign
In spight of all insulting Foes ,
He Conquers all where e'er he goes.

Printed for P. Brooksby, J. Deacon, J. Blare, J. Back.

pessimism returned. He would gladly have avoided a battle; as it was, he had planned his retreat and sent off some of his artillery even before the battle started. William, on the other hand, was full of confidence. He ignored Schomberg's pleas for caution; well aware of his superior numbers and fire-power, he decided to force a crossing at Oldbridge. To create a diversion, he sent Schomberg's son upstream with about a third of the army, with orders to cross and attack the enemy. Next day, 1 July, was hot and sunny. At first all went better than William could have hoped. The younger Schomberg crossed the river, and James, obsessed with retreat, sent two-thirds of his army to stop him from blocking the way back to Dublin. In fact, the two forces, separated by deep ditches, were unable to fight. Only one third of James's army, under Tyrconnel, was left to bear the brunt of the Williamite attack. William's Dutch blue guards were the first to cross, wading waist-deep under withering fire. Once they were over, the Irish infantry turned and fled but James's cavalry charged the Dutch guards again and again; 'my poor guards', William kept saying, but they held their ground and were joined by the Danes who had crossed a little further downstream. Finally, William led the cavalry across still further down; his arrival, at the head of the Enniskilleners, settled the issue. The Irish cavalry broke and fled. The retreat was prevented from becoming a rout partly by the rearguard action of the French cavalry and partly by William's failure to follow up his victory: presumably he did not want James to be captured. He need not have worried; James was back in Dublin that evening and hurried on towards France the next day.

William was left in possession of the field. He had lost about four hundred men, including the elder Schomberg; the Jacobites had lost rather over a thousand, including some prisoners and wounded who had been butchered by the English. Although he had fought fiercely, he had suffered no injury apart from a graze on his leg where part of his boot had been shot away. According to his doctor, 'He expressed neither joy nor any sort of vanity; only he looked cheerful.'

The Boyne was hailed in England and Europe as a great victory. It helped offset two great defeats; on land the French routed the allies at Fleurus while their naval victory at Beachy Head raised fears that they might invade England. The symbolic

'He expressed neither joy nor any sort of vanity'

importance of the Boyne was enormous – James had been driven out of Ireland for good – but its immediate military effect was less than William had hoped. He was able to march unopposed into Dublin, where the Protestants were ecstatic, 'blessing God for his wonderful deliverance as if they had been alive from the dead'. Any chance that the Jacobites might conquer all Ireland, remote since their failure to take Derry, now disappeared. But their army had not been destroyed; it now fell back on the Gaelic stronghold of Connaught, defending the line of the Shannon. William was to find that it was one thing to win a battle in the field but quite another to take towns as strongly fortified as Limerick or Athlone. Moreover, once their backs were to the wall, the Irish infantry fought with a bitter determination which had been sadly lacking at the Boyne. As a result, the war which William thought had been effectively ended at the Boyne was to drag on for well over a year.

In an effort to end the war quickly, William issued a declaration at Finglas on 7 July; he promised pardon to all common soldiers, labourers and artisans who surrendered by 1 August, but there was to be no mercy for the 'desperate leaders of the rebellion' unless they took great steps to convince William that they deserved it. The declaration was a serious error; its uncompromising tone made the Jacobites more intransigent, while the attempt to divide the men from their officers failed miserably and reflected ignorance of the social ties which bound them together. William soon found out that the war was not yet over, when he tried to take Limerick. There were about fourteen thousand Irish troops in the town and William's force of twenty-five thousand was not really adequate for a full-scale siege. Before his siege train could arrive from Dublin it was blown up by Patrick Sarsfield at Ballyneety. More guns were brought and a breach was opened in the walls, but an attempt to storm it was repulsed; the inhabitants, including women and children, showered the besiegers with great stones and broken bottles. Over 2,300 Williamites were killed or wounded. Next day, 28 August, it rained heavily; William feared that his guns would sink in the mud and raised the siege. A few days later he returned to England. He had tried to take Limerick that summer in the hope of ending the war; his failure to do so ensured that the war would go on for another year.

The battle of the Boyne: contemporary English print.
Victory was William's on 1 July 1690.

The rest of the story is soon told. Later in 1690 Marlborough led a quick and successful expedition against Cork and Kinsale, which elicited a barbed compliment from William: 'No officer living who has seen so little service as my lord Marlborough is so fit for great commands.' In 1691 the Williamite army was commanded by the Dutchman Ginckel; on 30 June he took Athlone and on 12 July he won the bloody battle of Aughrim. But Limerick held out, sustained by hopes of reinforcements from France, which eventually sailed, too late, on 13 October. The siege dragged on into September and Ginckel thought seriously of abandoning it for the winter; then, at the end of the month, the French still had not come and the Jacobites decided to negotiate. The treaty of Limerick was signed on 3 October. The military articles, which were punctiliously observed, offered a free passage to France for any soldier who wanted one, with transport provided by the English government; this reflected William's eagerness to bring the war to an end, even at the cost of providing Louis XIV with more troops (some twelve thousand in fact). The civilian articles were more ambiguous and less well observed. One allowed the Catholics the same religious privileges as they had enjoyed under Charles II, provided that they were consistent with the laws of Ireland; William and Mary undertook to try to secure further safeguards for them when the Irish Parliament met. Other articles promised security of life and property to Jacobite officers and men who submitted to William's government, and to civilians in Limerick and in areas occupied by the Jacobites at the time of the treaty.

William tried to administer the civilian articles fairly; he was usually punctilious in such matters and he had the feelings of his Catholic allies to consider. But the Irish Protestants had other ideas. Their desire for revenge was mixed with fear that the Catholics might rise again and receive further assistance from France. The guarantees given to the Jacobite officers and those under their protection were whittled down and Catholic proprietors lost nearly a million acres, reducing their share of the land to fourteen per cent. The promises of toleration were ignored completely; new penal laws decreed that Catholics should be disarmed and that their bishops and regular clergy should be banished. Finally an act of 1704 made it impossible for

OPPOSITE James on horseback at the battle of the Boyne. His defeat signalled the effective death of the Jacobite cause; two years later Louis XIV planned an invasion to restore him, but the hapless Stuart's hopes were dashed by the French defeat at La Hogue. A contemporary engraving.

144

The Royal Salutation,

OR,

The Courtly Greeting between K. *William* and Qu. *Mary* at his Return
from the Wars in *Ireland* to his Royal Pallace.

Tune is, I often for my Jenny strove.   Licensed according to order.

Queen.

WHen brave King VVilliam of renown
   came from the sharp and bloody scene,
Riding in triumph to the Town,
   for to embrace his Gracious Queen,
She was greatly then rejoyced,
   Lords, and all the Princely train;
This is a blessing, I'm possessing,
   for to see my Lord again.

The Irish Rebels felt thy Rage,
   which Romanists did not deny;
Unable they were to ingage,
   ut straight unto the Bogs did flye:

When this joyful News arrived,
   Protestants rejoyc'd amain;
And now a blessing, I'm possessing,
   to embrace thee once again.

King.

Said he, My noble Army bold,
   ne'r valu'd the insulting Foe;
But fought like noble Hearts of Gold,
   true English Courage they did show:
Falling on like Men undaunted;
   Charging through the Front and Rear:
Still as we fir'd, they retir'd,
   thus the coast we soon did clear.

Catholics either to buy land outright or to pass their estates on intact to their heirs. As a result, many of the Catholic gentry sank into poverty, while others turned Protestant. By 1776 only five per cent of the land was in Catholic hands, and Catholics (and Presbyterians) were completely excluded from political power. The completeness of the Protestant ascendancy was shown in 1715, when the Jacobite risings in Scotland and England aroused no echo in Ireland. After that, Irish Protestants became more concerned about their subordination to the English Parliament than about the quiescent Catholic majority.

William III remains to this day a cult figure among the Protestants of Northern Ireland, who still toast the 'glorious memory' of the man who saved them from 'Popery, brass money and wooden shoes'. For William, however, Ireland was never more than a remote and rather tedious sideshow, 'as it were out of knowledge of the world'. His main concern was to get it over as soon as possible so that he could get back to the serious business of fighting the French on the Continent; having defeated the Jacobites, he tried, without success, to restrain the Protestants' lust for revenge. His great importance in Irish history is due less to the Boyne, important as it was, than to his invasion of England in 1688. If James II had remained on the English throne, there was little to stop the Catholics from taking Derry and Enniskillen and so seizing all Ireland. As it was, William was able to use the resources of England to reconquer Ireland; once he made up his mind to do so, the issue could not be in doubt (although it might have been very different had Louis XIV been willing to pour more men and money into Ireland). So the Irish Protestants were saved, after having been in far greater peril from the Papists than the English ever were; thanks to William they were able to preserve their dominance for more than another century.

OPPOSITE A songsheet with a ballad describing the reunion between William and his Queen on his return from Ireland, with alternate verses allotted to each.

6 King

and Queen 1690-4

FROM THE START, William and Mary found life in England strange and uncongenial. William had brought England into his great struggle against France but he was to pay a heavy price in terms of ill-health and unhappiness. Both of them found the formal side of monarchy particularly irksome. The position of stadholder was a very functional one and William brought the same attitude to the English monarchy. He disliked the ceremonial and magical aspects of kingship; he refused to touch for the king's evil (scrofula) or to wash the feet of the poor on Maundy Thursday. He was obviously bored by the pomp of the coronation and later sneered at the 'foolish old Popish ceremonies'. His shyness and poor breathing made him shun crowds and Mary shared his feelings: 'My heart is not made for a kingdom and my inclination leads me to a retired life, so that I have need of all the resignation and self denial in the world to bear with such a condition as I am now in.' In Holland their Court had been small and private; they had moved mostly within a small circle of servants and close friends and, like most Dutch couples, they took a close interest in domestic details, planning improvements in their houses and gardens. In most royal Courts, however, whether they were chaotically informal, like that of Charles II, or rigidly formal, like that of Louis XIV, kings and queens led an intensely public existence, with the nobility and even casual sightseers watching their every move. This William and Mary could not stand, so under them the monarchy became more withdrawn and domestic. William liked to receive visitors privately, in his study or bedchamber, which they entered and left by the back stairs. His love of privacy did not increase his popularity, but it was what he and Mary wanted and it helped keep them sane. At times William did try to be more accessible and sociable, but he much preferred to go hunting at Windsor or Richmond; each autumn he spent several weeks at Dieren, recuperating after the summer's campaign. Mary passed her time as she had done in Holland, at prayers or at cards; she read as much as her poor eyesight would allow and spent much time supervising the rebuilding of their houses.

In her building schemes she co-operated closely with Sir Christopher Wren. At Hampton Court they planned to knock down all the Tudor buildings except the great hall and to

An English earthenware
dish, dated 1690, showing
Queen Mary surrounded
by allegorical figures.

replace them with an elegant, symmetrical palace and formal
gardens in the Continental manner. Her own favourite retreat
was the 'water gallery', by the river; there she could read, gossip
and enjoy the open air. The building went on quickly during
Mary's lifetime, but after her death William lost interest. At
Kensington Wren added four new pavilions to the original
house, which some thought made it look rather patched. In
1689 Mary was in great haste to get the rebuilding finished, but
Wren pressed on too fast and three workmen were killed when
a roof collapsed; two years later the south wing burned down.
Mary saw these disasters as God's punishment for 'the vanities I
was most fond of, that is ease and good lodgings'. Both she and
William spent much time on their gardens; William supervised
the waterworks and fountains while Mary chose the flowers,
shrubs and trees, including (of course) orange trees. Their
example naturally helped set new fashions: for neat, well-
proportioned redbrick houses, for geometrical gardens, for

evergreen shrubs (especially laurels) and for the blue and white
china which Mary collected so avidly.

However much William and Mary might have wanted to
devote all their time to their houses and gardens, they had other
tasks, more urgent and less pleasant. William spent each campaigning season abroad: in Ireland in 1690, in the Netherlands
in 1691–7. He knew that he alone could hold the alliance against
France together. Louis XIV may not have wanted a major war

152

INGSINGTON.

Kensington Palace in the reign of William and Mary. This contemporary print shows the symmetry of the gardens. Mary had considered herself fortunate in 'the convenience of my house and the neatness of my furniture' until the fire which took place in the summer of 1691.

and he may have suspended building operations at Versailles and melted down some of his household plate to help pay for it: but his armies were still formidable. He at least held his own in the Rhineland, Italy and the Mediterranean, but his main effort was concentrated in Flanders. There his forces outnumbered the allies' for much of the war and William, as so often, was reduced to trying to limit French gains. In the bloody battles of Steenkerk (1692) and Landen (1693), William did no better than

Hampton Court and William and Mary

William and Mary lavished special care on Hampton Court, spending a great deal of money on the building and the gardens. Mary threw herself wholeheartedly into 'examining and surveying the Drawings, Contrivances and whole Progress of the Works'. Grinling Gibbons provided wood carvings for Mary's suite and her bath was of white marble. As at Kensington, the work did not advance without accident, for here too some workmen were killed.

ABOVE A view of the south and east fronts of Wren's Hampton Court.
LEFT Part of the panelling on the King's staircase at Hampton Court.
RIGHT Long water: the wrought iron balcony looking out over the Thames.

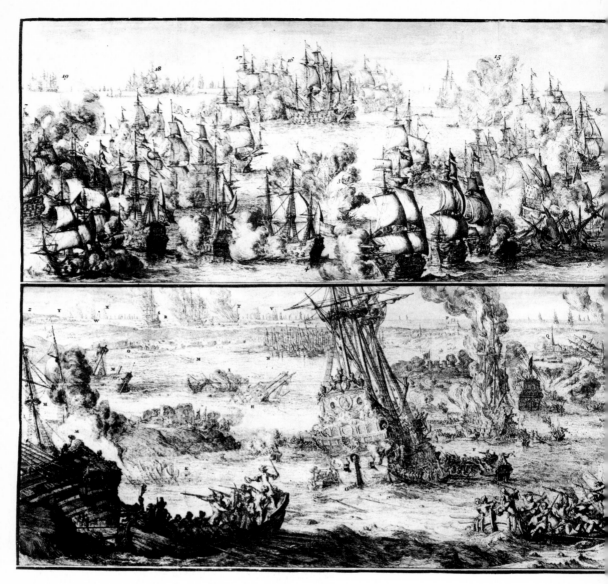

draw; both were seen by the English as defeats, but they prevented the French from advancing on Liége or Brussels. By
1694 the French economy was buckling under the strain; the
greatest French generals and administrators had now died, while
the Dutch and English armies improved each year. In 1694
William's forces outnumbered the French for the first time and
he was able to contain them without difficulty. In 1695 came his
greatest military feat; he took the prodigiously well-fortified

The battle of La Hogue in 1692, in which Admiral Russell defeated the French fleet decisively, though the victory was not followed up by the English and Dutch.

town of Namur, even though there was a strong French army available to relieve it. Namur gave him a reputation as a great general; more than any other event, it was to induce Louis XIV to make peace.

While William was abroad, Mary presided over the regency council that ruled England. She had no experience of government and disliked the thought of it: 'I must hear of business, which being a thing I am so new in and so unfit for, does but break my brains the more and not ease my heart.' William allowed the council as little initiative as possible: anything that could wait for his return was not to be dealt with. Mary was soon faced with great problems. After the French naval victory at Beachy Head in 1690 there were great fears of a French invasion, and a raiding party actually landed at Teignmouth. In 1692 there were again fears of invasion, which ended abruptly with Russell's great victory at La Hogue. Meanwhile, rumours of Jacobite plots were everywhere and the regency council was divided, its members being keener to attack each other than to do the King's business. In 1691 Mary wrote that she found 'a general peevishness and silliness in them all, except Lord Sidney' – and the charming Sidney was, alas, not much of an administrator. She was forced, therefore, to rely on Nottingham, widely known as 'Dismal'; 'I incline to have a good opinion of him,' wrote Mary, but added, 'It may be his formal grave look which deceives me.' Nottingham was honest and prepared to do his best, but his naval administration was less than brilliant and was vitiated by a long and bitter feud with Russell.

Mary's initiation into government was an ordeal, but she did a difficult job rather well. She had considerable common-sense and obeyed William's instructions to the letter; she could also show considerable initiative; in 1692, hearing rumours of disaffection among the officers of the fleet, she wrote to assure them that she was convinced of their loyalty; their conduct at La Hogue showed that her trust had been well-founded. After her first experience of government in 1690, she was able to write: 'The only thing that pleased me was that my husband was satisfied and told me that he was very much pleased with my behaviour.' Nevertheless, she missed William terribly:

I never do anything without thinking now, it may be, you are in the greatest dangers, and yet I must see company upon my set

157

days: I must play twice a week; nay I must laugh and talk, though never so much against my will. ... In this I don't know what I should do, were it not for the grace of God which supports me. I am sure I have great reason to praise the Lord while I live for this great mercy, that I don't sink under this affliction; nay that I keep my health; for I can neither sleep nor eat.

She longed to go back to Holland, 'to see again a country which is so dear to me and people with whom I have lived so long, so happily and with such contentment'. She even began to think of death: 'I do not know what will happen to me but, life being so uncertain, I prepare myself for death. I bless God that the only thing which makes death uneasy to me is that some might suffer for it.'

When William was in England, she was much happier, 'believing it very unnecessary for me to meddle or trouble my head when the King was here'. There were only two aspects of public life which always concerned her. William's handling of ecclesiastical affairs had lacked either skill or tact and he soon left them to Mary. Church patronage was controlled by Mary, Nottingham and Archbishop Tillotson; the bishops they appointed were mostly moderates, neither very High nor very Low Church, men of good character, competent preachers and conscientious pastors; there were no more rabid Whigs like Burnet. Secondly, Mary was very concerned with the improvement of morals and manners. Coming from sober, orderly Holland she thought England was full of debauchery and profanity. As regent she issued proclamations ordering the proper observance of the sabbath and urged magistrates to clamp down on drunkenness and swearing; she even had exhortatory letters read from the nation's pulpits. She tried to persuade her guards to attend church regularly, and William rebuked a young man who swore in his presence, saying that the Court should set a good example to the nation. The moral tone of the Court improved dramatically after the open sexuality of Charles II's time and James II's furtive and seedy affairs with unattractive women. (Burnet wickedly wondered if James's mistresses had been given to him by his priests as a penance.) True, William still had Betty Villiers living close to Kensington, but she kept discreetly out of sight. The 1690s saw a reaction against the easy-going obscenity of the Restoration period,

A portrait of John Tillotson, Archbishop of Canterbury, after Kneller. A gifted preacher, he had endeared himself to William many years earlier by loaning him some money just before the Prince and Mary embarked for Holland after their marriage.

which found expression in the numerous societies for the reformation of manners and in tracts like Jeremy Collier's *Short View of the Immorality and Prophaneness of the English Stage* (1698). Many of the leading figures in this movement were the conscientious divines whom Mary was promoting in the Church, and it clearly drew much of its strength from the Queen's patronage and example.

Another source of great unhappiness to Mary was her rapidly deteriorating relationship with her sister. At first, all went well; when Anne had a son, the Duke of Gloucester, in 1689, she tactfully called him William Henry. But friction soon developed. Anne was sluggish and taciturn and did not respond to

159

Jeremy Collier: engraving by E. Cooper after Lely's painting. Dryden found his condemnation of the dramatists' vices so accurately detailed that he concluded that the divine 'read them not without some pleasure'.

Mary's lively chatter. She was also dominated by the singularly unpleasant Sarah Churchill, now Countess of Marlborough, and her inordinately ambitious husband. One contemporary described the 'blemishes' of Sarah's character: 'Ill-grounded suspicions, violent passions and a boundless liberty of expressing resentments without distinction, from the Prince [George] downwards, and that in the most public manner and before servants.' Anne was a stupid, stubborn woman, but her quarrel with Mary would have been far less serious had it not been for Sarah's malign influence. The quarrel started with a petty squabble about some apartments at Whitehall which Anne wanted and which had been promised to someone else. Then

160

Marlborough's friends secured from Parliament a generous allowance of £50,000 a year for Anne, from which the Marlboroughs naturally benefited; this annoyed William and Mary, both because Parliament was much slower to vote the King money and because they had not been told of the proposal. When the oafish but inoffensive George went with William to Ireland, William refused even to have him at his table; he also refused to allow George to accompany him to Flanders in 1691.

The real break came at the end of 1691. Marlborough demanded the command of the English land forces in the next campaign. He alleged that William had too many foreign generals and that he was biased against Englishmen; he tried to stir up the English officers to support his claims. William had no intention of promoting him. Great general though he later became, he as yet lacked the experience for high command. His low birth told against him: many Continental generals were princes and would not speak to one of lower social rank. William also hated him for deserting James in 1688: 'Though he had himself profited by his treason, he abhorred the traitor.' Now, to make matters worse, Marlborough was in contact with James's Court at Saint Germain. Above all, William would not allow his control over military appointments to be challenged, for he believed that if he lost control of the army, he would be halfway to losing his throne. In January 1692, therefore, Marlborough was dismissed from all his offices.

A few days later Anne appeared at Court with the disgraced general's wife at her side. Mary was furious; she ordered Anne to dismiss Sarah and to leave her lodgings at the Cockpit; Anne refused to part with her favourite and moved to Sion House. The breach was now complete. Mary failed to visit Anne during the last, very painful stages of her latest pregnancy. When Anne refused yet again to dismiss Sarah, Mary wrote angrily: 'I cannot change my mind but expect to be complied with.' Anne replied, 'Sure never anybody was so used by a sister.' Although there was still some contact between William and George, the two sisters never spoke to each other again. It was a sordid, tetchy quarrel from which no one (except perhaps George) emerges with any credit; Mary showed a haughtiness and vindictiveness which were most unusual for her and which helped to make the breach irreparable. Burnet remarked that

OVERLEAF LEFT William at the time of his marriage: this portrait of 1677 is after Lely.
OVERLEAF RIGHT Wissing's portrait of Mary as Queen, in her royal robes.

QUEEN MARY.   WISSING

Mary was an ardent collector of china and loved to show visitors her cabinets full of it. Her enthusiasm spread to the English people and china-collecting became a national pastime.

RIGHT This tulip vase was probably designed by Daniel Marot for Mary's suite in the Water Gallery at Hampton Court, in 1694.

BELOW A model cradle in red earthenware, decorated with brown and white slips and glazed: Staffordshire, c. 1700.

'Both had engaged themselves before they had well reflected on the consequences of such a breach.' If either ever did reflect, they did so when it was too late.

The years after 1689 were a time of adaptation to new conditions. The Revolution settlement, and the failure to grant the King an independent income, ensured that the King had to learn to rule with Parliament; he had to manage Parliament, and politicians had to learn to work together in the public interest, to acquire a certain responsibility and an understanding of the problems of government. In addition, the war, the largest England had ever seen, enormously increased the volume of government business; this imposed great strains on an administrative and fiscal system which differed little in structure from that of the Middle Ages, despite recent improvements. The corruption and inefficiency which were normal features of Stuart administration now appeared on a far larger scale. And yet England not only survived but won the war and, in the process, developed the system of taxation and government borrowing which was to underpin British expansion in the eighteenth century. Much of the credit for this belongs to the King's ministers and administrators; much also belongs to William himself.

If William exercised considerable power, this was due less to his prerogative, large though it still was, than to his control of several key administrative departments. William was an excellent administrator and was prepared to work very hard. As a result he came to know more about the workings of several departments than any of his ministers or civil servants, which gave him considerable freedom of action. In these chosen areas, he was very reluctant to delegate responsibility and used heads of department as little more than clerks. He took good care that nobody knew all the secrets of his government, not even his confidential personal aides, Portland and Keppel; he wrote many of his letters himself. He wanted a dominant position in the administration, partly to preserve his freedom of action and partly because he knew from experience that he could not trust others to do the job properly. His standards of efficiency and integrity were very high and he soon became convinced that if he wanted important tasks to be done properly he would have to do them himself – and he was usually right.

A Delftware wig-stand. Late seventeenth century.

A silver gilt teapot made in London in 1685.

The departments William controlled were those directly relating to the war effort, which was always his main concern. From the start, he kept foreign affairs in his own hands, using the Dutch diplomatic corps, because few Englishmen had any experience of diplomacy. After Schomberg's disastrous expedition to Ireland, William took over the administration of the army; in 1693 he assumed responsibility for naval affairs as well, although he knew little about them. Finally, he extended his activities into the Treasury; he did not much care how the money was raised, so long as it came in; his main concern was to see that it was used properly for the war. But however great his dominance of the administration might be, he depended on Parliament for money. In order to get it, he had to descend into the political jungle and learn the arts of Parliamentary management.

William was not well equipped to deal with Parliament. He had little time for representative bodies or politicians; he regarded them as dilatory, inefficient and venal. He was not a

The Morgan Tankard. It was made by George Garthorne, a silversmith of Carey Street, on Queen Mary's instructions. It was then presented to Captain Janszoon Hartevelt as a token of gratitude for saving William's life, through his skilful navigation during the stormy crossing to Holland in 1691 for the congress at The Hague.

man to tolerate opposition or fools, and was usually too convinced of his own rightness to excel at the delicate art of compromise. But as always his authoritarianism was held in check by his realism. He might fume at the asinine and bloody-minded behaviour of his Parliaments, but they were a fact of life and he had to live with them. The means of doing so were outlined in a letter from Sidney and another in 1690:

It is without question impossible for a king of England to do any considerable thing in a House of Commons without a formed management; and by that we mean a number of men on whom the King may confidently rely, joined with the speaker (who now is most certainly yours), and they to meet privately every night and there to resolve how and by what methods they will oppose anything which may obstruct his Majesty's affairs, or propose anything that will further his interest the next day; amongst these there ought to be had at any rate two or three gentlemen who have fair reputations in the House, ... who must by no means have any employments during the sessions but be rewarded afterwards.

In short, careful planning and firm leadership were required, backed up by rewards of jobs or cash for those who behaved themselves. Such techniques were traditional, but the situation was now complicated by the existence of parties, groups of men united by common interests, principles or prejudices. If one party commanded a majority in the Commons, the King and his political managers would have to secure the co-operation of its leaders. The leaders would usually demand, as the price of their support, that the King should pursue policies which they liked and that he should admit certain of their friends to office. If the King did so, his freedom of action would be limited and they would be encouraged to make further demands.

The problem was to secure the support of a majority in Parliament without being dominated by the party leaders. Under Anne the problem was to be greater, as Parliament was divided between Whigs and Tories; there were few moderates or habitual supporters of the government. Under William the situation was more complex and fluid. The number of moderates and uncommitted was greater and there were three main groupings rather than two. The Tories hated William for his usurpation and his treatment of the Church. Their traditional loyalty to the Crown was, therefore, firmly suppressed and they made all the trouble they could while waiting for Anne's accession. There were also two groups of Whigs. The Country Whigs were the heirs of the opposition to Charles II. Obsessed with the corrupting effects of power, they attacked governmental mismanagement and corruption and watched constantly for attempts to extend the prerogative or influence of the Crown. Prickly and negative, they found that they had much in common with the Tories; for much of William's reign, Tories and Country Whigs worked together until they became almost indistinguishable. The Court Whigs, on the other hand, were more constructive; their leaders, nicknamed the Junto, showed themselves to be able administrators, but they were greedy for power and tried hard to impose their policies and friends on the unwilling King. None of these party groups, therefore, was entirely acceptable to William. All threatened to curtail his powers and limit his freedom of action; the Tories and Country Whigs were also liable to make vicious personal attacks on him. Managing such men was not going to be easy.

168

In 1690 William found himself with a mainly Tory ministry, led by Nottingham. It soon became clear that it was pitifully short of administrative and debating talent, and it fell back increasingly on crude bribes, handed out either by the Marquis of Carmarthen (formerly Danby) or even by William himself. By the end of 1692 the ministry's position was desperate. Russell's victory at La Hogue removed the threat of invasion, and the Tories began to argue that William's apparent failure at Steenkerk showed that the land campaign was a huge waste of men and money. They wanted to concentrate on attacking France at sea and in the colonies, which would, of course, be much cheaper. This forced William to reconsider his attitude to the two parties. He still regarded the Whigs as thinly disguised republicans and the Tories as the natural supporters of monarchy; but the Court Whigs had what the Tories lacked, cohesion and men of talent, and both they and the Country Whigs were committed to winning the war. William therefore began to heed the words of a new adviser, the Earl of Sunderland. Sunderland, having been James's chief minister, was quite free of party ties; he was also an astute politician and he developed a certain public spirit in his old age. He told William that however much he might loathe the Whigs, he had to work with them: 'It was very true that the Tories were better friends to monarchy than the Whigs were, but then his Majesty was to consider that he was not their monarch.' He wrote later:

> The great mistake that has been made ... has been to think that they [Whigs and Tories] were equal in relation to this government, since the whole of one may be made for it and not a quarter of the other ever can. Whenever the government has leaned to the Whigs, it has been strong; whenever the other has prevailed, it has been despised. ... I may be believed in this matter for the Whigs make me weary of my life and I would give half of what I am worth that it were otherwise.

In 1693 William took Sunderland's advice. He appointed some Whig ministers, while Sunderland coached his spokesmen and agents in the Commons; he went through lists of the members of both houses and considered how to persuade men to support the King's policies. Lord Brandon wanted to be made a general, Lord Mulgrave wanted a marquisate. Sunderland

Robert Spencer, Earl of Sunderland, the shrewd and unscrupulous statesman who had been Lord President of the Council in James's reign. William respected his informed appraisal of political situations and made him Lord Chamberlain in 1697.

hoped to persuade the Earl of Bath to discipline his sons, who sat in the Commons, by delaying payment of his pensions and the renewal of his lord lieutenancies. His aim was not to advance the interests of any party but to bring together all who were prepared to support the King: 'What does it matter', he drawled, 'who sarves his Majesty so long as his Majesty is sarved?' He and the new Whig ministers weeded out the dis-affected from the lower levels of the administration. The results in the next session were encouraging; the ministry suffered no major defeat. Even William was mollified when the charming but diffident Duke of Shrewsbury agreed to take office, which saved the King from having to speak to the more radical Whigs. Parliament seemed to have been brought under control, but it was not to last.

At Kensington, on 20 December 1694, Mary began to feel ill. Her health had been poor for some time, but she sensed that this was more serious; she put her papers in order, burning those she did not wish to be found. By the 22nd she was clearly ill; her doctors at once diagnosed smallpox. William, whose parents had both died of the disease, broke down; 'He burst into tears', recalled Burnet, 'and cried out that there was no hope of the Queen: and that from being the happiest he was going to be the miserablest creature upon earth.' He insisted on having a camp-bed moved into Mary's room; the lack of fresh air impaired his own health and his continual weeping upset Mary. By the 25th, however, she seemed so much better that the doctors began to think that she might have had measles, but that night her condition worsened markedly, and the Archbishop of Canterbury, Dr Tenison, told her to prepare for death. She felt little pain and was surprised that she did not even feel ill. On the 27th she took the sacrament and bade farewell to William; she weakened gradually and died at about one in the morning on the 28th. Her body was embalmed and lay in state at Whitehall. Her state funeral on 5 March was a magnificent affair and cost over £50,000. William, according to custom, did not attend.

Mary had had little fear of dying and had prepared herself calmly and methodically. She told Tenison that 'She thanked God she had always carried this in her mind, that nothing was to be left to the last hour; she had nothing then to do but to look up to God and submit to His will.' Burnet thought that 'She seemed to desire death rather than life.' Although she was only thirty-two, she already felt old: 'I believe that I am becoming old and infirmities come with age.' She died almost universally loved and respected; she was always far more popular in England than William. William told Burnet that 'During the course of their marriage he had never known one single fault in her.' The Tory diarist Evelyn wrote: 'In sum she was an admirable woman, abating for taking the crown without a more due apology, as does, if possible, outdo the renowned Queen

The Royal Hospital, Greenwich, an imposing monument to William's naval war: a view of the chapel dome and the Queen Mary colonnade. The hospital was built to ensure provision for disabled pensioner seamen. Construction began in 1696 and finished in 1752.

The Queene Leving in State who departed this life the 28 day of
december 1694 to the great greefe of all good Subiects.

With mourning pen, and melting eyes,   Our loss is her eternal gain,
with bleeding heart, and sobbing Cries,   and yet we cannt but Complain,
here lament the loss of one,   as having lost the sweetest Queen,
who was the brightness of the throne.   as ever in the Realm was seen

Printed and sould by Ioh: overton att the White horse without newgate

Elizabeth.' She had led a life of blameless rectitude and exemplary piety; if she was sometimes priggish and censorious, her motives were usually pure and unselfish: her treatment of Anne was perhaps the exception which proves the rule. She disliked politics and shunned responsibility, but when need arose, she had governed with courage and common sense. Her abilities were mediocre compared with those of her husband but her constant love and moral support had helped him to use his talents to the full. She fulfilled those tasks of monarchy which William disliked or was bad at, the social and the ceremonial. The fact that she was English and James II's daughter had enabled the revolutionaries of 1689 to preserve the outward appearance of continuity. Like William, she was essentially selfless and her ambitions were subsumed in his. For that reason she should be remembered less for her own limited achievements than for her contribution, intangible though it might be, to those of her husband.

OPPOSITE Mary lying in state: a contemporary engraving. William's grief was echoed throughout the country – and in Holland, too. The Viennese envoy to London wrote: 'It is impossible to describe the desolation which this death has caused to the whole nation. . . . The love which everyone had for the Queen is indescribable.'

Hampton Court

One of William and
Mary's favourite English
residences, largely
reconstructed by Wren.

RIGHT The elegant
Fountain Court.

RIGHT The ceiling of the
King's Bedchamber,
painted by the Italian
artist Antonio Verrio. It
shows Endymion asleep in
the arms of Morpheus.

LEFT The King's
Bedchamber, with its rich
red hangings.

7 William Alone

1695-1702

WILLIAM WAS PROSTRATED with grief at Mary's death. He collapsed at her bedside, and Portland had to carry him to bed. He was unable to sleep or even walk. On the 31st he received the condolences of Parliament but broke down when he tried to reply. It was almost a month before he began to recover and for a long time he was subject to sudden fits of weeping. He found it hard to accept that Mary was gone: 'I feel that I should be going to have supper with her this evening as usual,' he told Portland one day. He came to see Mary's death as a punishment for his sins: 'He turned himself much to the meditations of religion and to secret prayer,' wrote Burnet approvingly, 'The archbishop was often and long with him; he entered upon solemn and serious resolutions of becoming, in all things, an exact and an exemplary Christian.' He attended prayers twice a day and broke with Betty Villiers, who before the end of 1695 married Lord George Hamilton. William was also reconciled with Anne. When she came to see him, 'She told his Majesty in faltering accents that she was truly sorry for his loss, who replied he was much concerned for hers: both were equally affected and could scarcely refrain from tears or speak distinctly.' William gave Anne St James's Palace and accorded her a place of honour as heir apparent. George was admitted to the Privy Council, and Marlborough was restored to favour. Only occasionally was there friction; when James II died in 1701, Anne was angry that William did not order the Court to go into full mourning. When William died a few months later she made it clear that she was in mourning for her father, not for her brother-in-law.

Gradually William's life returned to normal. He lived mostly at Kensington, hunting at Richmond or Windsor at the weekends. His attention became concentrated more and more on English affairs, partly because they were more complicated, partly because England was emerging as the major partner in the alliance and partly because he could safely leave Dutch affairs in the capable hands of Pensionary Heinsius. Meanwhile, William's health gradually deteriorated. He was especially troubled by swellings in his legs; always a bad patient, he never gave his doctors' dubious remedies a chance to work. Disgusted by the obstreperousness and chauvinism of the English, he found it a relief to go on campaign each year; even after the war ended, he

178

WILLIAM. REX

MR ANTONI HEINSIUS,
Raad-Penfionaris van Holland.

N. Pothoven naar 't Origineel van G. v. d. Eikhout by den Heer Burgem. van der Heim te Rotterd.

Antonius Heinsius, Grand Pensionary of Holland:
an engraving by Claatsens. After 1689 he
effectively governed Holland in William's absence.

180

still went over to hunt at Dieren. Perhaps because he was depressed, he began to eat and drink more than in the past and he became irritable and gloomy. He relaxed only in the company of his Dutch friends with whom he would drink far into the night. He never remarried, although he occasionally considered it for purely diplomatic reasons; nor is there any record of a mistress after Betty was married off. He lived more than ever in the all-male environment which he had always preferred; when he needed a hostess, he asked Anne.

There was one important change among those closest to him. In 1691 his attention had been drawn to Keppel, one of his pages, when he broke his leg in a hunting accident: 'That is such a good lad, he withstood terrible pain,' remarked William. By 1695 it was clear that Keppel was supplanting Portland in William's favour. It is probable that it was simply Keppel's youth and charm which made William prefer him to the stolid and ageing Portland: he made an old man feel younger. But Keppel's rather effeminate good looks soon gave rise to rumours that his relationship with William was a homosexual one. This cannot be proved or disproved but it seems unlikely. William himself was not highly sexed and had a strong sense of sin, while Keppel was heterosexual to the point of being randy. William was both annoyed and saddened by the rumours: 'It seems to me very extraordinary that it should be impossible to have esteem and regard for a young man without it being criminal.' As William showered favours on Keppel (he was created Earl of Albemarle in 1696), Portland grew increasingly resentful; the two favourites often quarrelled and once almost came to blows. After 1697 Portland spent much of his time on embassies abroad; he finally resigned his offices in 1699, and Albemarle reigned supreme. He was less hard-working than Portland but performed similar functions as a confidential personal assistant to the King.

The war of 1689–97 was the greatest in which England had ever engaged; somehow it had to be paid for. Taxation under William was heavier than ever before; fifty-eight million pounds were raised in taxes in thirteen years. (James II, by far the most affluent of the Stuarts, had an annual revenue of about two millions.) A wide range of new taxes was introduced, including excises on salt and various types of alcohol, and the

Much controversy has centred around William's relationships with men. The two courtiers most often singled out for rumours of the King's homosexuality were William Bentinck, created Earl of Portland on William's accession to the English throne, and the younger Arnold Joost van Keppel, created Earl of Albemarle. These portraits show the superficial similarity in their looks.

LEFT Portland: a portrait from the studio of Rigaud. RIGHT Keppel, painted by Kneller.

land tax. This last was assessed more accurately than previous direct taxes and brought in about a third of the money raised by taxation; rates soon rose as high as four shillings in the pound. But all these taxes were still insufficient and so the government had to resort to borrowing, and it was there that the greatest advances were made in the 1690s.

In the seventeenth century it took a long time and cost a lot of money to collect taxes. When kings needed money in a hurry (as they often did), they borrowed for short periods and at high interest. As they were often slow to repay the money, their credit was often shaky. In the early years of the war, Parliament placed a similar reliance on short-term loans to meet immediate

183

needs. As it became apparent that the war would last some time, people came to realise that such short-term loans merely ensured that the nation's financial problems would be even worse in a couple of years' time. Parliament therefore did two things to improve the position. First it declared all debts incurred during the war to be 'debts of the nation', and pledged itself to repay them. This greatly strengthened the government's credit, made investors more willing to lend and helped keep interest rates within bounds. Secondly, it began to consider ways of raising long-term loans and voted particular taxes for long periods to provide money to pay the interest on them. As England had no experience of such long-term borrowing, Parliament was open to suggestions from 'projectors', like the remarkably inventive Scot William Paterson. The expedients which were tried included state lotteries and a tontine, in which, as the original contributors died off, the annuities paid to the survivors became larger and larger. Gradually the system of borrowing was rationalised. At first, individual departments raised loans as they needed them, Parliament assigning part of the revenue to service each one. It eventually became accepted that a deficit on any departmental fund should be made good from others and in 1697 an Act established a general consolidated fund, or sinking fund, to make good the deficits on the various funds. It was still assumed that the debts would eventually be paid off.

The most important innovation of all was the Bank of England. The moving spirits behind it included Paterson and the Chancellor of the Exchequer, Charles Montagu. The Tonnage Act of 1694 set aside the revenue from a duty on beer, ale and vinegar to service a loan of £1,200,000. The Crown incorporated the subscribers as a bank and allowed them to deal in bullion and bills of exchange. The Bank, whose first home was Powis House in Lincoln's Inn Fields, soon made further loans to the government and helped it to weather the serious financial crisis of 1695–6. The men of the 1690s had to experiment and improvise in an effort to cope with financial problems of unprecedented size. Inevitably there were mistakes and failures, and one should not overestimate the government's successes; interest rates were seldom below eight per cent and were often as high as fourteen. Nevertheless, the achievement was considerable and laid the foundation of the more sophisticated credit apparatus of the eighteenth century. Even more remarkable was the fact that, even while the war was going on, the Mint was able to buy in worn and clipped coins at face value and replace them with milled coins of the proper weight. The short-term financial effects were dire – trade slumped and William could raise hardly any money for the 1696 campaign – but in the long run England was provided with the sound coinage that was essential for a healthy economy. As it was, the development of long-term credit enabled England to emerge from the wars far less exhausted than France, a country with a much larger population and much greater resources; the growth of the London money market prepared the way for London to replace Amsterdam as the financial capital of Europe.

William himself seems to have played little constructive part in these developments. His role was limited to attempts to provide enough money for the war and to limit Parliament's interference in fiscal and economic matters. His main concerns, as always, were war and diplomacy. When Mary died, he did not at first feel like continuing the struggle, but his spirit soon returned and in 1695 he took Namur. Louis was now ready to make peace, but naturally wanted to get the best possible terms. He was always trying to persuade members of the alliance to make a separate peace and in 1696 he succeeded with the Duke of Savoy. William too was ready for peace. The Flanders campaigns of 1696–7 ended in stalemate. It took some time to fix terms and to persuade Leopold to agree to them, but peace was signed at Ryswick late in 1697. Louis abandoned all that he had taken since 1678, except for Strasbourg and part of Alsace, and he recognised William as King of England, thereby, by implication, abandoning his support for James II's claims. This represented a humiliating defeat for the hitherto invincible Louis and raised the prestige of William, as architect of the alliance, to its apogee.

At home, things went less well. The Whigs whom William had brought into the ministry proved greedy and hard to control. Wharton and Montagu in particular wanted to push out the remaining Tories and moderates and to replace them with Whigs. They therefore began to attack governmental corruption, a subject bound to arouse the interest of the perennially

185

The Bank of England

Founded in 1694 to finance William's war against Louis XIV, the Bank of England was opposed by the Tories, who feared that it would be dominated by Whig financiers who would grow rich at the public expense and use their wealth to dictate to the government. To guard against the monarchy becoming absolute, the Bank was forbidden to lend money to the Crown without consent of Parliament.

RIGHT William Paterson, a leading promoter, and one of the first directors of the Bank of England.
A bronze bust by Charles Wheeler.
BELOW The first few entries in the original subscription book of the Bank.

36	London the 28th day of June 1694	
1164	J. De Mallonos for Mrs Lewis de Vareilla of St James Westminster Widow doe subscribe summe of ffive hundred pound	500
1169	J Matthew Kenrick for Mris Elizabeth Parker of Woaden Spinster doe subscribe three hundred pounds	300
1165	J Thomas le Heup for Michall de la Sugannere of Rotordam Cash doe subscribe One hundred & fifty pounds	150
1166	J Thomas le Heup for Mris Mary de Kherenc of London Spinster doe subscribe one hundred & fifty pounds	150
1170	J Edward ... of St Martin in ye ffeilds Esq. Doe subscribe One hundred pound	100
1167	J Thomas le Heup for Lewis francis Petit of London Esq doe subscribe Two hundred pounds	200
1168	J Thomas le Heup for Nicholas de Louvigny of London Esq. doe subscribe one hundred pounds	100
1171	J John ... doe subscribe One hundred pounds	100
1172	J Joshua Baring of London Merchant Doe subscribe ffive hundred pounds	500
1173	J Humphry Seymor for Edward Littleton of Westminster Esq do subscribe one thousand pound	1000
1174	J Joseph Hardey of London Linen Draper doe subscribed Two hundred pounds	200
1175	J Peter Leddell for Dame Ann Andrewes of Walton in Surrey doe subscribe Two hundred pound	200
1178	... of London Warehouseman doe subscribe ffive hundred pound	500
1176	... Stanton of London Clothworker doe subscribe One hundred pounds	100

ABOVE The Royal Charter
of Incorporation of 'The
Governor and Company
of the Bank of England'.

suspicious backbenchers. In the investigations that followed, the reputations of Carmarthen and of the Speaker of the Commons were blasted and one of Sunderland's agents was sent to the Tower for taking a bribe. The Whig ministers hated Sunderland and did not see why they should do the hard work of pushing government measures through the Commons while Sunderland distributed all the rewards. Meanwhile, it was clear that, without Mary, William was even less popular than before. During the last years of his reign, unscrupulous politicians proved increasingly ready to exploit the Commons' xenophobia and to make easy political capital out of attacks on the Dutch King and his Dutch favourites. William's triumphs abroad were to be in sad contrast to repeated defeats and humiliations at home.

With the end of the war, the need for national unity seemed to disappear. Resentment of high taxes now burst to the surface and was intensified by unusually high food prices. Parliament soon showed that it was in a vindictive mood. Using the argument that a standing army in peacetime could become an instrument of despotism, it ordered that the army should be cut to just over seven thousand men; it also insisted that these should all be British, so William had to send home his beloved Dutch blue guards. 'By God,' he is said to have remarked, 'if I had a son, they should stay.' He regarded the disbanding of most of the army as criminally stupid when war might break out at any time over the Spanish succession; Parliament, he said, had done in a day what Louis XIV had been unable to do in eight years. He again considered abdicating; Burnet found him furious at the ingratitude of the English:

*'By God, if
I had a son, they
should stay'*

> He doubted whether he could carry on the government after it should be reduced to so weak and so contemptible a state. He said that if he could have imagined, that after all the service he should have done to the nation he should have met with such returns, he would never have meddled in our affairs; and that he was weary of governing a nation that was so jealous as to lay itself open to an enemy rather than trust him, who had acted so faithfully during his whole life, that he had never once deceived those who trusted him. He said this, with a great deal more to the same purpose, to myself: but he saw the necessity of submitting to that which could not be helped.

188

He got little help from his ministers. In the post-war atmosphere of disillusionment and recrimination, they were out to grab what they could and to save themselves; one by one they cut their losses and resigned. William for his part made little effort to get on with them; he refused to speak to Montagu and would not give office to Wharton. All was confusion. 'People in Parliament now occupy themselves with private animosities and party quarrels and think little of the national interest,' wrote William sadly in 1698, and later: 'It's impossible to credit the serene indifference with which they consider events outside their own country.' The obstructiveness of Parliament and the disbanding of the army gravely weakened William's bargaining position in the diplomatic manœuvres of 1698–1701; it was fortunate that he could fall back on his prestige as conqueror of Namur.

In the years after the peace of Ryswick, the central problem in international relations was the Spanish succession. Carlos II was a grotesque creature, the ultimate product of Habsburg in-breeding. His jaw stuck out so far that his two sets of teeth could not meet and he had to swallow his food whole; he was also mentally retarded. It was amazing that he had survived so long and he could not be expected to live much longer. There were three main claimants to the succession: Louis XIV's second grandson, Philip of Anjou; Joseph Ferdinand, the son of the Elector of Bavaria; and Leopold's younger son, the Arch-duke Charles. It was a moot point which of the three had the best claim; it did not really matter, since the issue was bound to be decided by diplomacy or force rather than by strict legal right.

The situation was both complex and delicate. Leopold's victories in the east had made him almost powerful enough to counterbalance the power of France. If the bulk of the Spanish empire (which included the southern Netherlands, Milan, Naples, Sicily and vast areas in the New World) went to either Philip or Charles, it might disastrously upset the European balance of power. On the other hand, both Louis and Leopold were emerging from long, exhausting wars, and Louis for one had no wish to embark on another. The way was therefore open for compromise; if the compromise was to work, it needed the approval of William, who could speak for both England and

Holland. William, deprived of his army, was equally anxious that a compromise should be reached. He believed that he could do nothing to stop Louis from seizing the whole Spanish empire, so that all he could do was to limit his gains as much as possible. In fact, William's view of Louis's ambitions (and especially of his designs on the Spanish Netherlands) was out of date. Louis had long since abandoned his dreams of universal empire, and his recent defeat had been a chastening experience. Besides, Louis thought of France's position in European terms while William's strategic thinking was largely limited to the Netherlands.

In relation to the Spanish succession, Louis's position was very complicated. He regarded his grandson's claim as valid, but realised that in practice the Spanish and French crowns would have to remain separate; the Spaniards would not agree to assimilation into France. If Philip became King of Spain, therefore, the glory of the Bourbon family would be greatly enhanced, but France would gain little or nothing: indeed the French might have to waste blood and money defending the decrepit Spanish empire. On the other hand, if the major powers agreed to partition that empire, France might gain territories of the greatest strategic value; at the very least, Louis could prevent Leopold from getting too much. The terms which Louis agreed with William in the first partition treaty (October 1698) were surprisingly moderate. They showed clearly that Louis's main concern was defence against the Emperor; he was not interested in the Spanish Netherlands which, with Spain and the colonies, were to go to the neutral candidate, Joseph Ferdinand. The Austrians were to get the strategically vital territory of Milan and, to balance this, the French were to get Naples and Sicily. Louis's letters to his negotiators show clearly the reason for his moderation; he was afraid of provoking another war and another coalition against France.

Unfortunately for all concerned, Joseph Ferdinand died early in 1699; there was now a straight contest between Bourbon and Habsburg for the succession. Louis and William signed a second partition treaty in March 1700, by which Charles was to have Spain and the Spanish Netherlands while Philip was to get the Spanish possessions in Italy. Louis's aim was clearly to

Carlos II of Spain, with his prominent Habsburg jaw. On his will hinged the question of the Spanish Succession, not finally resolved until 1715.

separate the two branches of the House of Habsburg. Leopold refused to accept the treaty, and the situation changed when Carlos II died in November; his will declared that the whole Spanish empire should go to Philip of Anjou. Louis was taken completely by surprise. He now faced an agonising choice: should he try to persuade Leopold to agree to the partition or should he claim the whole empire for his grandson under the terms of the will? Either way, it might lead to war; he eventually decided to abide by the will, and was soon at war with the Austrians. It was by no means certain that either the Dutch or the English would enter the war, but Louis undertook a series of provocative actions which more or less forced them to fight. This was odd, because he did not want a general war, nor did he

191

The Emperor Leopold I:
one of the major
participants in the
continuing contest with
Louis XIV. An engraving
after Bloem's portrait.

prepare for it; one can only assume that his judgment was not what it had once been. He provoked the Dutch by sending French troops to occupy the 'barrier fortresses' in the Netherlands, which the Spanish had allowed the Dutch to garrison after Ryswick.

The English were even less willing to fight. Parliament continued its vendetta against William. There were bitter attacks on his grants to Portland and others of lands confiscated from the Irish Jacobites; a bill to revoke these grants was 'tacked' to the land tax bill; if the Lords and King wanted to reject it, the King would have to go without his money. In 1700 Anne's last surviving child, the Duke of Gloucester, died; the Act of Settlement of 1701 settled the succession after Anne in the House of Hanover; it also imposed a variety of limitations on the powers of the future foreign King which showed the Tories' hatred of the present one: he was not to leave England without Parliament's consent, no foreigner was to hold any office or receive any land from the Crown, and so on.

With Parliament in this mood, William was unlikely to find much sympathy for his foreign policy. The Commons was now dominated by Tories, and Sunderland urged William to appoint some Tory ministers, in the hope that he could instil some sense into them once they were in office; but to no avail. There was a great outcry when details of the partition treaties became known; the Tories feared that they might lead to war, and they had had enough of wars. The Commons claimed that it should have been consulted; to emphasise the point, the House impeached four of the King's ministers for their alleged part in making the treaties. Carlos II's will was welcomed in England, as it seemed to remove the danger of war. Even when Louis began to behave provocatively, the Commons were still very reluctant to antagonise him by openly preparing for war. Gradually, however, the pressure of public opinion began to make itself felt, in pamphlets, petitions and the rumblings of the London mob. In September 1701, when James II died, Louis recognised his son as James III of England, which further inflamed public opinion. By the end of the year, William was sufficiently confident of the outcome to hold a general election. The new House of Commons was evenly divided between

A Dutch punchbowl commemorating the peace of Ryswick in 1697. At The Hague, Dutchmen celebrated with a firework display, much to the pleasure of the visiting Tsar of Russia.

Whigs and Tories, but even the Tories now appreciated the need to prepare for war. William's speech at the opening of Parliament on 31 December captured the new mood of Parliament and nation. Burnet recalled:

> He laid it upon them to consider the dangers they were in and not to increase these by new divisions among themselves; ... he expressed a readiness to forgive all offences against himself and wished they would as readily forgive one another so that no other divisions might remain but that of English and French, Protestant and Papist.

He stressed too that Parliament had a European responsibility:

> The eyes of all Europe are on this Parliament; all matters are at a standstill till your resolutions are known. ... If you do in good earnest wish to see England hold the balance of Europe and to be indeed at the present head of the Protestant interest, it will appear by your right improving the present opportunity.

By the start of 1702, then, William had at last secured a Parliament that could be relied on to prosecute the coming war vigorously. By 1701 his health was failing. The swellings in his legs grew worse and he was sometimes unable to walk. For some time he had been unable to control a really spirited horse. He assumed that the coming war would be a long one and that he would not live to see it through; he would certainly be too frail to lead his troops into battle. He therefore took steps to ensure that the war would be carried on as he would have wished. The calling of a co-operative Parliament was one step. More important, he began to groom his successor as architect and chief diplomat of the anti-French coalition. The leading negotiators of the 1701 Grand Alliance were Heinsius, for the Dutch, and Marlborough, for the English; Marlborough's favour with Anne made him very much the coming man. William, tactfully, kept out of the way; he felt that the terms of the alliance should be fixed by those who were to fight under it. His concern that England and her allies should be in a position to fight and win the coming war gave the lie to his repeated assertions that he did not care what happened after his death. He had no heirs to think of and lacked personal ambition; but he served an ideal, that of defending Europe against French aggression. That ideal lived on after his death; that it did so owed much to William himself.

In February 1702 William's health was beginning to recover after the rigours of winter. Then on the 21st his horse stumbled on a molehill in Richmond Park, and he fell and broke his collar-bone. (Malicious Jacobites later drank many toasts to the mole, 'the little gentleman in the velvet coat'.) He seemed reasonably well afterwards, but he could take little exercise and his legs swelled. On 4 March he suddenly felt weary and fell asleep on a chair. He grew weaker and found it difficult to eat. By the 7th he had a fever and was clearly very ill. He was in great pain but his senses remained clear and he accepted the imminence of death with his usual calm and fatalism: 'I am drawing towards my end,' he said simply. He had told Portland 'that he knew death was that which he had looked at on all occasions without any terror; sometimes he would have been glad to have been delivered out of all his troubles, but he confessed now he saw another scene and could wish to live a little longer'. Early on the 8th he received the sacrament, gave the keys of his cabinet to Albemarle and prepared to die. He bade farewell to all and died shortly after eight o'clock. When his body was opened, the lungs were found to be shrivelled and rotten. He was also found to be wearing a ring and a lock of Mary's hair around his neck.

His death occasioned little sorrow in England. 'No king can be less lamented than this has been,' noted one contemporary, 'even by those that was his greatest admirers in his lifetime ... the very day he died, there were several expressions of joy publicly spoke in the streets – of having one of their own nation to reign over them.' In her first speech to Parliament, Anne pointedly stressed that her heart was 'entirely English'. Unlike his wife, William was buried privately, almost furtively, at midnight. It had been argued that it would be wrong to spend large sums on a state funeral when the nation would soon be at war; it was planned to erect a statue instead, at a later date. Burnet was sceptical: 'Some years must show whether these things were really intended, or if they were only spoke of to excuse the privacy of his funeral, which was scarce decent, so far was it from being magnificent.' In death as in life, the English would not accord William the respect he deserved.

'The little gentleman in the velvet coat'

8
The Achievement

'THE DEPRESSION OF FRANCE was the governing passion of his whole life': thus Burnet described the obsession which dominated William's actions for over thirty years. He saw French aggression, military and commercial, as a constant threat to the freedom, religion and prosperity of Holland, England and Europe. For much of his life, his analysis of Louis's intentions was correct. In 1672 Louis set out to smash the power of the Dutch; in 1683, when the Turks were at the gates of Vienna, he even had dreams of becoming Holy Roman Emperor. But behind Louis's aggression, there always lurked an element of fear. From 1688, as Leopold became more powerful, Louis's attitude was fundamentally defensive and was dominated by exaggerated fears of being attacked by the Habsburgs. In 1688 and in 1701–2 Louis did not want a major war and was not prepared for one; that major wars did in fact occur can be explained partly by circumstances, partly by Louis's own miscalculations and partly by the fact that his earlier behaviour had convinced the other powers that he was an incorrigible aggressor.

If William's analysis of Louis's motives was not always correct, the wisdom of his policies was also sometimes open to question. His stubborn refusal to make peace between 1675 and 1678 harmed the Dutch more than the French and they were not unreasonably reluctant to make war in 1683–4 in response to Louis's aggression far away in the Rhineland; at times in this period, William seems to have been irresponsibly trigger-happy. On the whole, however, William's inflexibility and single-mindedness did the anti-French cause far more good than harm; they helped him to rally the Dutch in 1672 and to build and maintain the coalitions of 1673–8 and 1689–97. Long before William became King of England, Louis regarded him as his most dangerous enemy; when he conceded defeat for the first time at Ryswick, he knew full well that it was William alone who had made that defeat possible. He even accorded William a grudging respect while, according to an Englishman in Paris, Louis's courtiers called him 'the finest prince in the world'.

The attitude of the Dutch to William's memory is mixed. On one hand he saved the republic in 1672; he also converted the Dutch army from an undisciplined rabble with corrupt and cowardly officers into one of the best fighting forces in Europe.

This greatly improved army enabled the republic to defend itself until Louis XIV's France no longer threatened its very existence. The financial cost of this was very heavy and by the 1720s the republic was a second-class power. This cannot altogether be blamed on the wars or on William. The republic's ascendancy had always been a little precarious and artificial. It had emerged to prominence in a power vacuum; Spain was rapidly decaying while France, weakened by internal disorders and a series of royal minorities, had yet to realise its full potential. On the economic side, when countries like France and Britain, with larger populations and greater resources, began to copy Dutch techniques, the Dutch ascendancy could not long be maintained.

Some Dutch historians, like Professor Geyl, have argued that William's rule damaged the republic in two ways. He and his Court have been blamed for the increasing French influence on all aspects of Dutch life – dress, manners, literature, architecture and art. This seems to treat as a peculiarly Dutch phenomenon something that was happening throughout Europe: everywhere France was the dominant cultural influence. It seems

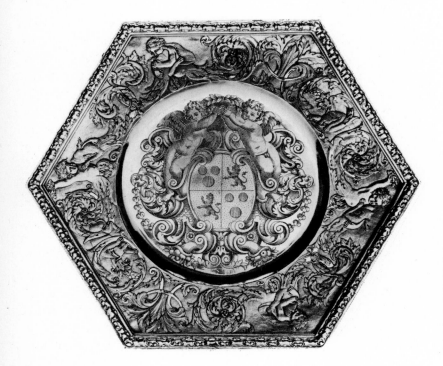

A silver gilt waiter bearing the mark of Benjamin Pyne, the London goldsmith. It is engraved with the arms of Sir William Courtenay, of Powderham Castle, Devon, who died in 1702.

unreasonable to blame William for this, especially bearing in mind the great influx of Huguenots into the republic in the 1680s. The second criticism is more convincing, that William's regime had a harmful effect on Dutch political life. The purge of the regent oligarchies after the revolution of 1672 excluded William's enemies from power in most towns, though not in Amsterdam. In the years that followed, William's main concern was to secure the regents' co-operation or acquiescence in

The end of the seventeenth century saw the increase of French influence on all aspects of culture in other European countries, perhaps more so in Holland than in England. These engravings of 1689, by J.D.de St Jean, show the current French fashion for dressing 'incognito':
LEFT The 'man of quality', his cloak covering the lower half of his face.
RIGHT The 'woman of quality', holding a mask to her face.

his foreign policy. He was not fussy how this co-operation was obtained and some of his agents, like Odijk or Dijkvelt, were far from scrupulous. The Dutch political system depended very much on the integrity and public spirit of the regents; this alone prevented the town councils from becoming corrupt and selfish oligarchies. Under William, much of this public spirit and integrity was eroded. Gradually a system of contracts grew up, whereby regents were guaranteed their places in return for

promises of unconditional obedience to the stadholder. In each town a few families came to monopolise the places on the council and the perquisites which went with them; the door was no longer open to talented newcomers. Much of the responsibility for this sapping of public spirit must lie with William. His singleness of purpose and European outlook gave him little sympathy with the give-and-take and parochialism which were at once the weakness and the strength of Dutch politics. It is possible that standards of public conduct would have declined anyway; as dangers from outside diminished, so would a sense of common interest and common purpose. It is also true that without William the republic might not have survived at all. But it is clear that, under William, the erosion of the old republican virtues accelerated. If this was the price that the republic had to pay for survival, it was a heavy one.

William's achievement in Ireland was simple. He completed a process which had been going on for almost a century, whereby the Protestant minority gained a monopoly of power over the Catholic majority. William had no interest in re-imposing Protestant domination in Ireland for its own sake; he was a tolerant man, and his servants and agents included Catholics and even Jews. He invaded Ireland to prevent Louis from using it as a base from which to attack England. When the war looked like dragging on into 1692, he was glad enough to offer generous terms to the defenders of Limerick; it was not his fault that the Irish Protestants would not let him keep his word. Ireland to William was of only peripheral importance; it is ironical that the country which least interested him should be the one where his name is most remembered.

It was on England that William left his greatest mark, through the Revolution of 1688. It could not have happened without him, for nothing short of a full-scale invasion could have driven James out. The Revolution led to great changes in English government and politics and in England's place in the world; its impact on English economic, social and intellectual history is not unimportant. All in all, it did far more to change the course of English history than the greatly overemphasised events of 1640–60. This is not to suggest that these changes were intended either by William or by the men who supported, or acquiesced in, his seizure of the crown. Far more of the changes stemmed from the wars which were a direct consequence of the Revolution than from the Revolution settlement. Nevertheless, the Revolution's achievements were remarkable enough. In an age of absolutism, it helped to create a comparatively liberal political system in a comparatively free society, which was to be the wonder of eighteenth-century Europe – not least because it worked.

It is easier to say what the Revolution led to than to say what it prevented. In considering this point, one has to face an unanswerable question: would the campaign to pack Parliament have succeeded? If those whom James supported had been elected, would they have done his bidding when Parliament met? We cannot know, as the elections were never held. James thought that he would succeed; the opinions of contemporaries varied. I myself doubt if he could have got his way. If he did not, he would have had little alternative but to seek to recover the support of the Tories and to patch up the old alliance of Church and King (as he tried to do late in 1688). The monarchy would probably have survived much as it had been under Charles II: not absolute but much stronger than it was to be after 1688. Such a solution was certainly the aim of the Tory loyalists who tried to mediate between James and William in December 1688.

Most of James's subjects, however, did not see the situation in this way. Their paranoid fears of Popery and despotism temporarily overcame their abhorrence of rebellion and they looked to William for deliverance. Their motives were overwhelmingly conservative, to secure the ancient constitution and the Protestant religion against an innovating king. The men who made the Revolution settlement did not set out to produce a blueprint for the future. Living in a world where rapid technological progress and economic growth are accepted as both natural and necessary, it is hard for us to imagine the very different mental climate of the seventeenth century. The world was then far more static, and few as yet regarded 'progress' as either possible or desirable; the myth of the ancient constitution and the Common Law's reliance on precedent taught men to seek legitimacy and perfection in the past. In 1689 Parliament tried to patch up the ancient constitution and to get it working again with as few changes as possible. It is ironical that their

actions led to such great changes – greater changes, in fact, than those which followed the far more dramatic events of 1640–60. The fact that they did so was due less to the settlement itself than to the war and to the King's weakened financial position.

The constitutional settlement was significant in two ways. First, in the field of political theory, it made resistance an acceptable concept. In all relationships between a king and his subjects there always existed the ultimate sanction of forcible resistance; in 1688–9 that resistance had succeeded and had been hallowed by the law. This made it clear (if it had ever been in doubt) that kings had to exercise their powers within limits, a fact which was rationalised in theoretical terms by the fiction of the original contract. Secondly, the rule of law was established. Many constitutional conflicts of the seventeenth century can be explained by differing interpretations of the law and by the kings' exploitation of ambiguities or loopholes in the law to raise money, to harass their opponents or to pursue unpopular religious policies. After 1689 two important things happened. First, the subjects' interpretation of the law triumphed and it became accepted that Parliament, rather than the judges, should decide on politically contentious points. Secondly, the King ceased to use the courts for political purposes. Not until the Act of Settlement was it laid down that the King could not dismiss judges at will, but William in fact showed great restraint and did not interfere with the judges' independence. After 1689 the Common Law remained rather erratic and still imposed brutal punishments for minor offences against property; but it was free from political pressures and protected the individual and his property against the state.

With the King now dependent on Parliament for money and with the great increase in the number of rewards at his disposal, the influence (and not the prerogative) of the Crown became the main threat to Parliament's independence. Under William and Anne, the Crown's managers tried to maintain a balance between the parties, but in 1715 the Whigs swept to power and set out to crush the Tories; all the best places in the administration, the armed forces and the Church were henceforth filled with Whigs. It is another irony of the Revolution that it saved Parliament from being manipulated by the Crown only for it to be manipulated even more effectively a generation or so later

Wood carving at the end of the seventeenth century: ABOVE The figure of Ceres carved in oak.
LEFT The cherubs carved on the Dean's canopy in St Paul's Cathedral, by Grinling Gibbons.

by Whig politicians like Walpole and Newcastle. A pamphleteer of 1733 looked back at James II's campaign to pack Parliament and remarked: 'What pity ... the art of borough-jobbers had not been found out then to complete the king's scheme.' It is true that Parliament survived as an institution and later showed a great ability to adapt to changing circumstances. But this might have happened anyway. James II aimed to tame Parliament, not abolish it; if he had failed to tame it he would probably have been forced to maintain it, as part of a deal with the Tories.

When William invaded England, he had little interest in preserving either Parliament or the laws of England. He himself was authoritarian by nature and regarded representative bodies as slow, inefficient and corrupt. He had little time for the slow processes of the law and never understood why English law did not allow the use of torture to extract confessions. It is yet another irony of the Revolution that the man who made possible the extension of political liberty in England was responsible for curtailing political liberty in his own country.

William's aim was, of course, to bring England into the war against France. This he did, with very important results. In the sixteenth century England had been too poor to take on major powers like France and Spain, as Henry VIII found out to his cost. Elizabeth wisely avoided foreign adventures, and those she undertook were limited and ineffectual. In the seventeenth century England's wealth, especially commercial wealth, gradually grew but, because of Parliament's parsimony and distrust (justified or unjustified), the Stuarts were unable to tap this growing wealth in the form of additional taxation; they therefore usually could not afford a foreign policy. In 1689, however, England was forced into war with France; it was a simple matter of survival; if England did not fight, there was a real danger that James II would be restored by a French army. If Louis XIV had not underestimated England's importance, this might well have happened in 1690–1.

Once in the war, the English had to pay for it. Except in the period 1640–60, they had been taxed very lightly by Continental standards. Now they had to pay far more; they grumbled, but they were neither beggared nor starved in the process. (In England, unlike France, the burden of direct taxation fell most

heavily on those best able to pay.) Moreover, the development of long-term loans on security guaranteed by Parliament enabled the government to tap the wealth of the private investor. This ability to attract almost limitless loans from the public gave England its enormous financial advantage over France in the eighteenth century. France was a much larger and potentially much richer country, but the monarchy's credit was so bad that few would lend money and then only at exorbitant interest. The war then made England a major European power for the first time; the financial apparatus developed to meet the needs of the war was to enable England to intervene regularly in European affairs and to defend and extend its colonial empire.

Another result of the war, one where William's role was crucial, was the development of the British armed forces. The navy was in reasonably good shape in 1688, thanks mainly to Pepys; but constant vigilance was needed to keep it in good order; the members of the new Admiralty board were forever

The period after the Restoration saw the flourishing of drama as well as criticism of its morality.
ABOVE LEFT A scene from Congreve's comedy *The Double Dealer*, which appeared in 1694. The engraving is after Hayman.
ABOVE RIGHT A portrait of the playwright and architect Sir John Vanbrugh, after Thomas Murray. His major successes were the bawdy comedies *The Relapse, or Virtue in Danger*, the unfinished *The Provok'd Wife* and *The Confederacy*.

quarrelling, and William felt compelled to take over responsibility for naval affairs in 1693, although he knew little about them; he at least prevented the situation from becoming worse. His impact on the army was much greater. There had been no standing army before the Civil War; Cromwell's veterans were mostly disbanded in 1660 and Charles II's army was quite small. James II's was larger, but most of its members had seen little active service and many resigned or were dismissed at the Revolution. Within two years, an army of sixty thousand men had been raised. The men were mostly raw and undisciplined and the officers mostly had little experience and were more ornamental than useful. The officers, in fact, proved harder to train than the men and it is not surprising that William relied at first on foreigners and on those who had served in the British regiments in the Dutch service. Gradually, as with the Dutch army, William battered and bullied this unpromising material into shape. William lacked the genius of Marlborough, but he had great determination and was willing to work very hard, and was a better disciplinarian and military administrator than the great English general. His efforts laid the foundation on which Marlborough was later to build. It was William rather than

The opening bars of Henry Purcell's 'Golden Sonata' composed in 1683. The organist at Westminster Abbey and also of the Chapel Royal, he composed many odes to Queen Mary.

A contemporary engraving of Sir Thomas Osborne, Earl of Danby. He had supported the marriage between William and Mary, and in 1689 he became Lord President of the Council, and Marquis of Carmarthen.

Marlborough who made the English army formidable; without that army, England could not have become a major European power.

The effects of the war on English economic and social development were complicated. The boom in overseas trade of the 1670s and 1680s came to an abrupt end, mainly because of the disruption caused by the war, although the coinage crisis was another important factor. On the other hand, partly because of the decline in investment opportunities overseas, there was a great increase in financial speculation at home. The growth of government borrowing offered secure and lucrative investments. The demands generated by the armed forces helped make large fortunes for contractors. City financiers made a killing on the recoinage, buying in clipped coins and selling them to the Mint at face value. The fact that there were so much better chances than ever before of making a fortune in the City had important social and political consequences. Traditionally social status and political power had been intimately associated

209

Regulations passed at Drapers Hall, at a meeting of the General Assembly of the 'Subscribers of Land and Money towards a Fund for the National Land-Bank' on 14 December 1695. The Land Bank was a counterbalance to the Bank of England, but it failed through lack of support.

DRAPERS·HALL:
London, *December* the 14*th*, 1695.

At a General *Assembly* of the *Subscribers* of *Land and Money towards a Fund for the* NATIONAL LAND-BANK.

Ordered, THat no Subscriber of Lands, Tenements or Hereditaments, shall be a Director, or have a Vote in any General Assembly, who shall not by himself, or by his lawful Attorney to be appointed by him for that purpose, first subscribe an Instrument, a true Copy whereof is as follows, *viz.*

" WE whose Names are underwritten, Subscribers of Lands,
" Tenements and Hereditaments towards a Fund for the
" *National Land-Bank*, do hereby for our selves severally declare, That
" we will settle our said respective Estates to be part of the Fund of
" the said Bank, in order to be intituled to the Profits, and subject
" to the Losses and Charges thereof, if our said Estates shall be ap-
" proved and received to be part of the said Fund. And we do hereby
" respectively promise to *John Briscoe* of *London*, Merchant, that we
" will pay to him for the use of the said Bank, our proportionable
" Parts of all Losses and Charges already suffer'd and expended,
" and to be hereafter suffer'd and expended in erecting and carrying
" on the said Bank, until we shall respectively withdraw our said
" Estates, or our said Estates shall be refused to be admitted as part
" of the said Fund. In witness whereof we have hereunto set our
" Hands this 14th day of *December*, *Anno Dom.* 1695. and in the
" seventh Year of the Reign of our Soveraign Lord, *William* the
" third, by the Grace of God King of *England*, &c.

Ordered, That a Book for Money-Subscriptions be laid open at the Office of the said Bank, until the first Thursday in *Hillary* Term next, to compleat the Subscriptions for a Million of Money.

Ordered, That those Persons who have subscribed Money to the said Bank, and have not made their first Payment, shall be admitted to pay in both their first and second Payments on or before the fifth day of *January* next, according to their Subscriptions, for which they shall be allowed Interest for their whole Subscription-Money from the time of such Payment.

Ordered, That the Choice of 36 Directors be made upon the first Thursday in *Hillary* Term next, being the 23d of *January* 1695.

with the ownership of land. Successful business and professional men bought country estates, concocted bogus pedigrees and tried to marry their children into the gentry. Now, however, land was far less attractive as an investment than it had been at the start of the seventeenth century; agricultural profits were low and land (unlike ready money) could not be hidden away and so was heavily and accurately taxed. Meanwhile, small groups of financiers, especially the Bank of England, came to

210

wield far more effective power than any country gentlemen ever could.

The rise of this 'moneyed interest' caused the first serious cracks in a ruling class that had been pretty homogeneous in social and economic terms. Powerful corporations could now dictate terms to the government. Men who had made fortunes from trade, finance or public office also began to buy their way into Parliament, squeezing impecunious gentlemen out of boroughs which they and their families had represented for generations. The country gentlemen tried to hit back; in 1711 Parliament passed a bill excluding from the Commons all those who did not own land to a certain annual value; it proved a dead letter. Many landed gentry continued to sit in Parliament, but by 1715 they no longer possessed the overwhelming predominance that they had had before 1688. Land was still the main determinant of social status, but not the sole source of political power. In 1709 Henry St John, later Viscount Bolingbroke, sadly described the situation as he saw it:

> We have now been twenty years engaged in the two most expensive wars that Europe ever saw. The whole burden of this charge has lain upon the landed interest during the whole time. The men of estates have, generally speaking, neither served in the fleets nor armies, nor meddled in the public funds and management of the Treasure.
>
> A new interest has been created out of their fortunes, and a sort of property which was not known twenty years ago is now increased to almost equal to the *terra firma* of our island. The consequence of all this is that the landed men are become poor and dispirited. ... In the meanwhile those men are become their masters who formerly would with joy have become their servants.

The rise of the moneyed interest had not been foreseen or intended either by William or by the men who made the Glorious Revolution. Like the vast increase in government jobs, the partial disappearance of the landed MP with roots in his constituency was to make easier the erosion of Parliament's independence under Walpole and Newcastle. Other side-effects of the Revolution, equally unintended, were more beneficial. The Toleration Act and William's refusal to enforce the penal laws brought a virtual end to religious persecution in England. A few years later the censorship of the Press was abolished;

typically, perhaps, this was not the result of any belief in the desirability of the freedom of the Press for its own sake, but because the Commons resented the monopoly which the censorship gave to the Stationers' Company, which tended to delay publication and to push up book prices.

But if English society gradually became freer and more rational after 1688, this owed more to chance and force of circumstances than to a clearly formed belief in liberty. Men thought more of 'liberties', of local, group or personal privileges defined in legal terms, than of 'liberty' as a general ideal. But the freer world of post-Revolution England was soon to find philosophical justification in the works of John Locke – in *Two Treatises of Government, A Letter Concerning Toleration* and, above all, in *An Essay Concerning Human Understanding*. This last work revolutionised man's understanding of himself and of his place in society. Locke abandoned the traditional Christian teaching of the natural depravity of man, tainted as he was by original sin. Instead, he claimed that man's knowledge and values are acquired entirely by experience, by the operation of his senses as interpreted by his rational intellect. This theory made possible a much more optimistic view of man: he could be taught, improved, even made perfect. More than any other work, the *Essay* established the possibility of human progress within the world; it was a far cry from the traditional Christian view that the world was a vale of tears, to be endured and never improved, and that perfection could be found only in the after-life.

Locke's ideas had not, of course, developed in a vacuum. Over two centuries men like Copernicus, Galileo, Harvey and Newton had made the workings of the universe and of the human body less mysterious. This growing awareness that the universe functioned according to regular laws changed man's attitude towards God; the behaviour of the heavens was no longer seen as the expression of a harsh and inscrutable will; God was seen instead as the benevolent architect of a rationally ordered and smoothly functioning cosmos. The Church modified its teaching to take account of the new knowledge; it talked less of hell-fire and more of practical morality. Religion became less 'enthusiastic', more functional and rational. Men began to think less of what divided different kinds of Christians and more

John Locke: a portrait after Kneller. His philosophical and political writings provided a justification of the view of man as a rational being, especially in the context of the England of the 'Glorious Revolution'.

The house of Sir Isaac Newton (now demolished) in Blue Cross Street near Leicester Square: a nineteenth-century engraving. Newton made incredible advances in the fields of mathematics, physics, astronomy and optics. Wordsworth appraised him thus: 'a mind for ever/Voyaging through strange seas of Thought, alone'.

of what united them; the zeal to persecute those of different opinions gradually waned.

In William's reign the fact of change was obvious in English society; man's growing knowledge of the world made him increasingly confident of his ability to direct and hasten this change. It was a time of experiment and invention. Faced with unprecedented financial needs, the state had to improvise and experiment and there was no shortage of suggestions from the public. Aristocratic amateurs dabbled in science and tried to solve practical problems which once would have interested only artisans. The number of patents for new inventions, already large under Charles II, increased greatly after the

213

Revolution. The foremost minds of the age took an active part in government: Locke sat on the Board of Trade, Newton was Master of the Mint and the great statistician Gregory King was employed by the Treasury. The energy and the willingness to experiment which characterised the quarter century after 1689 had their roots in the Restoration period and before, and in the growth of European scientific thought over two centuries. Nevertheless, the Revolution accelerated their development; on one hand there were so many new problems to solve; on the other the Revolution, implicitly or explicitly, involved change and criticism of existing institutions; it also led to the removal of restrictions, ecclesiastical and governmental, on intellectual life. However, this energetic, questioning spirit did not influence those in power for very long. Once the gains of the Revolution were secure, conservatism replaced a desire for change among the nation's rulers. The potentially dynamic concept of the perfectability of man gradually gave way to a static, complacent view of the perfection of the existing order of things – all is well, 'whatever is is right'. Nevertheless, the concept of the feasibility of progress was established even if, in the age of Walpole and Newcastle, it became unfashionable among those in power; it was to re-emerge later in the eighteenth century.

One must beware, then, of seeing history as a simple linear progression from the dreadfulness of the past to the better world of the present. History, like life, is complicated. It is over-simplistic to see the Revolution as saving England from Popish despotism and making possible the growth of liberty and of Parliamentary government. There is, of course, some truth in this view. English politics and society became freer and more dynamic after the Revolution and not all the gains were lost under Walpole and Newcastle. There is still a certain plausibility in Macaulay's argument that England avoided a bloody revolution in the nineteenth century because it had had a bloodless one in the seventeenth. Nevertheless, it would be wrong to see the Revolution (as Macaulay does) as impelling England un-erringly in the direction of liberal democracy, just as it would be wrong to see the changes that followed it as either intended or foreseen: long-term trends, force of circumstances and sheer chance also played a major part. It is also certain that William, the prime mover of the Revolution, disliked many of its

OPPOSITE The graceful interior of the chapel of the Royal Hospital, Greenwich by Wren, looking towards the east end.

214

consequences, which were to make life difficult and unpleasant for him. Whether or not these consequences were intended, however, they happened, and some of them would not have happened without William. It is sad that the English, who have so many reasons to be grateful to William III, accord his memory less respect than it deserves.

No one doubted in the last quarter of the seventeenth century that William was one of the greatest men in Europe. His determination alone made possible the containment of Louis XIV in the 1670s and 1680s; in the 1690s he led the coalition which inflicted on the French what was to be the first of many defeats. As a hard, single-minded man he made many enemies. He was impatient of opposition and was often unscrupulous in dealing with it. He was also a shy man, whose personal contacts, except with soldiers and close friends, were often awkward and unsuccessful. As Burnet wrote:

> His designs were always great and good: but it was thought he trusted too much to that and that he did not descend enough to the humours of his people, to make himself and his notions more acceptable to them. This, in a government that has so much of freedom in it as ours, was more necessary than he was inclined to believe: his reservedness grew on him so that it disgusted most of those who served him.

Thus although, in his relationships with his wife and close friends, William could both show and inspire great affection, he never got on well with politicians. This embittered him 'which he did not take care enough to conceal, though he saw the ill effects this had upon his business'. This helps explain the apparent paradox that a man whose achievements were so great should have been so unpopular among those who had good cause to be grateful to him. Even Burnet was needled by him at times, but the Bishop had no doubt of William's place in history:

> I consider him as a person raised up by God to resist the power of France and the progress of tyranny and persecution. ... After all the abatements that may be allowed for his errors and faults, he ought still to be reckoned among the greatest princes that our history, or indeed that any other, can afford.

OPPOSITE
A contemporary tapestry portrait of William. Unlike his wife, he died unlamented, though his stature throughout Europe was not disputed.

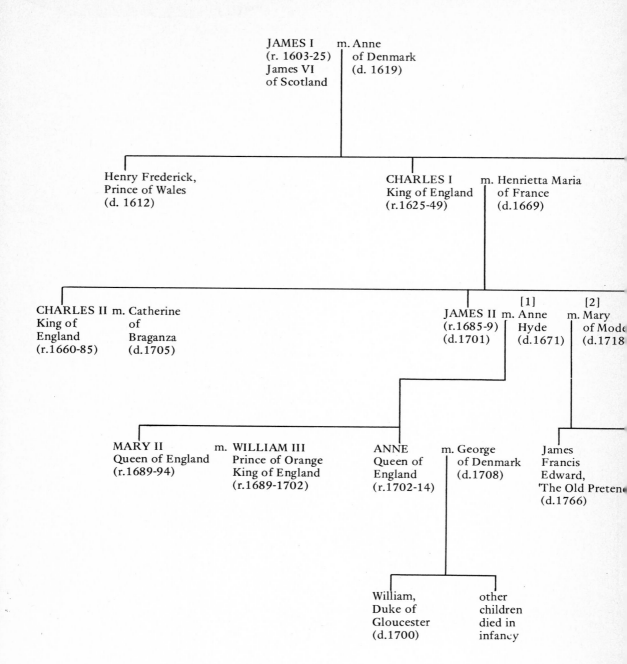

JAMES I
(r. 1603-25)
James VI
of Scotland

m. Anne
of Denmark
(d. 1619)

Henry Frederick,
Prince of Wales
(d. 1612)

CHARLES I
King of England
(r.1625-49)

m. Henrietta Maria
of France
(d.1669)

CHARLES II
King of
England
(r.1660-85)

m. Catherine
of
Braganza
(d.1705)

JAMES II
(r.1685-9)
(d.1701)

[1]
m. Anne
Hyde
(d.1671)

[2]
m. Mary
of Mode
(d.1718

MARY II
Queen of England
(r.1689-94)

m. WILLIAM III
Prince of Orange
King of England
(r.1689-1702)

ANNE
Queen of
England
(r.1702-14)

m. George
of Denmark
(d.1708)

James
Francis
Edward,
'The Old Pretene
(d.1766)

William,
Duke of
Gloucester
(d.1700)

other
children
died in
infancy

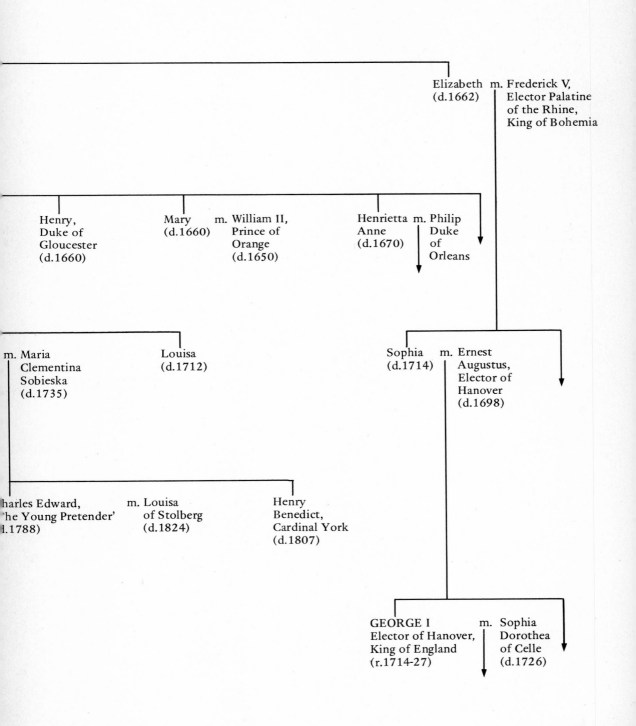

Elizabeth m. Frederick V,
(d.1662)   Elector Palatine
            of the Rhine,
            King of Bohemia

Henry,   Mary   m. William II,   Henrietta m. Philip
Duke of   (d.1660)   Prince of   Anne   Duke
Gloucester   Orange   (d.1670)   of
(d.1660)   (d.1650)   Orleans

m. Maria   Louisa   Sophia   m. Ernest
Clementina   (d.1712)   (d.1714)   Augustus,
Sobieska   Elector of
(d.1735)   Hanover
                                                              (d.1698)

harles Edward,   m. Louisa   Henry
he Young Pretender'   of Stolberg   Benedict,
d.1788)   (d.1824)   Cardinal York
                                       (d.1807)

                                       GEORGE I   m. Sophia
                                       Elector of Hanover,   Dorothea
                                       King of England   of Celle
                                       (r.1714-27)   (d.1726)

Select bibliography

Much the best life of William is that by Baxter, although he is sometimes less than fair to William's opponents. An asterisk indicates that a book is particularly recommended.

Ashley, M., *The Glorious Revolution of 1688* (1966)

Baxter, S.B., *William III* (1966)★

Beckett, J.C., *The Making of Modern Ireland, 1603–1923* (1966)★

Browning, A., *English Historical Documents, 1660–1714* (1953)
Thomas, Earl of Danby (1951)

Burnet, G., *History of My Own Time* (1823)

Carswell, J., *The Descent on England* (1969)
From Revolution to Revolution: England 1688–1776 (1973)

Clark, G.N., *The Later Stuarts* (2nd ed., 1955)
The Seventeenth Century (2nd ed., 1947)

Cragg, G.R., *From Puritanism to the Age of Reason* (1950)

Davies, G., *Essays on the Later Stuarts* (1958)

Dickson, P.G.M., *The Financial Revolution in England, 1688–1756* (1967)

Feiling, K.G., *History of the Tory Party, 1640–1714* (1924)★

Geyl, P., *The Netherlands in the Seventeenth Century, II. 1648–1715* (1964)★
Orange and Stuart, 1641–72 (1969)★

Grew, E. and M.S., *The Court of William III* (1910)

Haley, K.H.D., *The Dutch in the Seventeenth Century* (1972)
The First Earl of Shaftesbury (1968)
William of Orange and the English Opposition, 1672–4 (1953)

Hamilton, E., *William's Mary* (1972)

Hatton, R. and Bromley, J.S. (eds.), *William III and Louis XIV: Essays 1680–1720 by and for Mark A. Thomson* (1968)

Hazard, P., *The European Mind, 1680–1715* (1953)

Holmes, G. (ed.), *Britain After the Glorious Revolution, 1689–1714* (1969)

Holmes, G. and Speck, W.A. (eds.), *The Divided Society: Parties and Politics in England, 1694–1716* (1967)

Horwitz, H., *Revolution Politicks: The Career of Daniel Finch, Second Earl of Nottingham* (1968)

Jones, J.R., *Britain and Europe in the Seventeenth Century* (1966)
 The First Whigs (1961)
 The Revolution of 1688 in England (1972)★
Kemp, B., *King and Commons, 1660–1832* (1957)
Kenyon, J.P., *Robert Spencer, Earl of Sunderland* (1958)★
 The Stuart Constitution (1966)
Locke, J., *An Essay Concerning Human Understanding* (various editions)
 Two Treatises of Government, ed. P.Laslett (1960)
Macaulay, T.B., *History of England* (1849–61)
MacInnes, A., *Robert Harley* (1970)
Miller, J., *Popery and Politics in England 1660–88* (1973)
Ogg, D., *England in the Reigns of James II and William III* (1955)★
Plumb, J.H., *The Growth of Political Stability in England, 1675–1725* (1967)★
Pocock, J.G.A., *The Ancient Constitution and the Feudal Law* (1957)
Simms, J.G., *Jacobite Ireland, 1685–91* (1969)★
Straka, G.M. (ed.), *The Revolution of 1688* (1963)
van der Zee, H. and B., *William and Mary* (1973)
Western, J.R., *Monarchy and Revolution* (1972)
Williams, E.N., *The Eighteenth Century Constitution* (1960)
Wilson, C.H., *England's Apprenticeship, 1603–1763* (1965)
Wolf, J.B., *Louis XIV* (1968)★

Index

The Royal Salutation,

OR,

The Courtly Greeting between K. *William* and Qu. *Mary* at his Return
from the Wars in *Ireland* to his Royal Pallace.

Tune is, J often for my Jenny ſtrove.　　　　　Licenſed according to order.

Queen.

VVHen brave King VVilliam of renown
　　came from the ſharp and bloody ſcene,
Riding in triumph to the Town,
　　for to embrace his Gracious Queen,
She was greatly then rejoyced,
　　Lords, and all the Princely train,
This is a bleſſing, I'm poſſeſſing,
　　for to ſee my Lord again.

The Iriſh Rebels felt thy Rage,
　　which Romaniſts did not deny;
Unable they were to ingage,
　　ut ſtraight unto the Bogs did ſlye:

When this joyful News arrived,
　　Proteſtants rejoyc'd amain;
And now a bleſſing, I'm poſſeſſing,
　　to embrace thee once again.

King.

Said he, My noble Army bold,
　　ne'r valu'd the inſulting Foe;
But fought like noble Hearts of Gold,
　　true Engliſh Courage they did ſhow:
Falling on like Men undaunted;
　　Charging through the Front and Rear:
Still as we fir'd, they retir'd,
　　thus the coaſt we ſoon did clear.